DATE DUE

ILL 12-30-14

PATHOLOGY

SOLVING CRIMES WITH SCIENCE:
Forensics

Computer Investigation
Criminal Psychology & Personality Profiling
DNA Analysis
Document Analysis
Entomology & Palynology
Explosives & Arson Investigation
Fingerprints, Bite Marks, Ear Prints
Forensic Anthropology
Forensics in American Culture
Mark & Trace Analysis
Pathology
Solving Crimes With Physics

PATHOLOGY

Maryalice Walker

Mason Crest

Mason Crest
450 Parkway Drive, Suite D
Broomall, PA 19008
www.masoncrest.com

Printed and bound in the United States of America.

First printing
9 8 7 6 5 4 3 2 1

Series ISBN: 978-1-4222-2861-6
ISBN: 978-1-4222-2872-2
ebook ISBN: 978-1-4222-8958-7

The Library of Congress has cataloged the
hardcopy format(s) as follows:

Library of Congress Cataloging-in-Publication Data

Walker, Maryalice.
  Pathology / Maryalice Walker.
      p. cm. — (Solving crimes with science, forensics)
  Audience: 012.
  Audience: Grades 7 to 8.
  Includes bibliographical references and index.
  ISBN 978-1-4222-2872-2 (hardcover) — ISBN 978-1-4222-2861-6 (series) — ISBN 978-1-4222-8958-7 (ebook)
  1. Forensic pathology—Juvenile literature. 2. Criminal investigation—Juvenile literature. 3. Forensic sciences—Juvenile literature. I. Title.
  RA1063.4.W352 2014
  614.1—dc23
                          2013006964

Produced by Vestal Creative Services.
www.vestalcreative.com

Contents

Introduction   6

1. Early Death Investigation   9

2. Forensic Pathology: Where Scientists Dare to Tread   27

3. The Crime Scene   45

4. Examining the Body   57

5. The First Incision   73

6. The Cold Hard Facts: Victim Identity and Time of Death   83

7. Reconstructing the Crime   97

Glossary   107

Further Reading   108

For More Information   109

Index   110

Picture Credits   111

Biographies   112

Introduction

By Jay A. Siegel, Ph.D.
Director, Forensic and Investigative Sciences Program
Indiana University, Purdue University, Indianapolis

It seems like every day the news brings forth another story about crime in the United States. Although the crime rate has been slowly decreasing over the past few years (due perhaps in part to the aging of the population), crime continues to be a very serious problem. Increasingly, the stories we read that involve crimes also mention the role that forensic science plays in solving serious crimes. Sensational crimes provide real examples of the power of forensic science. In recent years there has been an explosion of books, movies, and TV shows devoted to forensic science and crime investigation. The wondrously successful *CSI* TV shows have spawned a major increase in awareness of and interest in forensic science as a tool for solving crimes. *CSI* even has its own syndrome: the "*CSI* Effect," wherein jurors in real cases expect to hear testimony about science such as fingerprints, DNA, and blood spatter because they saw it on TV.

The unprecedented rise in the public's interest in forensic science has fueled demands by students and parents for more educational programs that teach the applications of science to crime. This started in colleges and universities but has filtered down to high schools and middle schools. Even elementary school students now learn how science is used in the criminal justice system. Most educators agree that this developing interest in forensic science is a good thing. It has provided an excellent opportunity to teach students science—and they have fun learning it! Forensic science is an ideal vehicle for teaching science for several reasons. It is truly multidisciplinary; practically every field of science has forensic applications. Successful forensic scientists must be good problem solvers and critical thinkers. These are critical skills that all students need to develop.

In all of this rush to implement forensic science courses in secondary schools throughout North America, the development of grade-appropriate resources that help guide students and teachers is seriously lacking. This new series: *Solving Crimes With Science: Forensics* is important and timely. Each book in the series contains a concise, age-appropriate discussion of one or more areas of forensic science.

Students are never too young to begin to learn the principles and applications of science. Forensic science provides an interesting and informative way to introduce scientific concepts in a way that grabs and holds the students' attention. *Solving Crimes With Science: Forensics* promises to be an important resource in teaching forensic science to students twelve to eighteen years old.

1

Early Death Investigation

The soil was soft. Crime-scene investigators tramped through it, their shoes sinking silently into the rich earth. They dug the soil, searching for signs of human remains. Since 1983, more than sixteen women from Vancouver's "Low Track" district, most of them prostitutes, had mysteriously vanished. So far, investigators had searched the same site more than once, only to walk away empty-handed and baffled. The site, a fourteen-acre (5.6-hectare) pig farm in nearby Port Coquitlam, British Columbia, yielded no evidence that could tie the prime suspect, Robert Pickton, to the disappearances. Police did not even have a body or a definite crime scene to guide their investigation.

Then, in 1997, investigators interviewed a man named Bill Hiscox, who proved to be the breakthrough lead they had needed. Hiscox worked for Pickton's business, P&B Salvage in Surrey, just southeast of Vancouver. He told investigators a story that made the hair on their arms stand up.

Every month, Hiscox collected his paychecks at Pickton's "creepy looking" pig farm. Pickton and his brother often threw rave parties at the farm under the guise of a fraudulent charity organization, the Piggy Palace Good Times Society. According to Hiscox, Pickton kept a suspicious collection of purses and IDs in his trailer and often went to the Low Track district to visit prostitutes. Contrary to police expectations, however, the search of the farm that ensued failed to turn up any evidence against Pickton, and the list of missing women only grew longer.

Police finally caught up with Pickton that same year when Wendy Lynn Eistetter, a prostitute from the Low Track district, survived an attack at the farm. Despite multiple stab wounds, she escaped to the highway, where a passing motorist stopped and took her to the emergency room. Pickton was charged with attempted murder, but to investigators' alarm, he was released ten months later. Still more women disappeared.

By February of 2002, about fifty-four women were missing. Investigators had a pretty good idea Pickton was the culprit; they organized an exhaustive search of the farm. What they found made the community shudder. Apparently, Pickton had become sloppy in the few years since the last search of his property. Investigators found human remains packed into freezers next to pork carcasses and mixed with pork meat in wood-chippers. In May of that year, scientists uncovered remains of the first missing prostitute and identified her, using DNA analysis. More DNA samples collected at the farm matched those from family members of two other missing women. As time passed, scientists unearthed remains of thirty women whose DNA matched that of family members of missing prostitutes. At last, the worst serial killer in Canada's history was sentenced to life in prison, without possibility of parole for twenty-five years.

Arresting Robert Pickton and stopping him from taking more victims would have been impossible without dedicated scientists and the sophisti-

Robert Pickton was charged with fifteen accounts of first-degree murder after the remains of missing prostitutes were found all over his pig farm.

cated technology they use to capture criminals. If not for hundreds of years of experimentation in biology, chemistry, and medicine, technology such as DNA fingerprinting, which today is so common and critical to identifying victims and placing suspects at crime scenes, would not exist. The history of forensic pathology—the application of medicine to the law—is the story of advances in both criminal investigation and medicine, that together use tales of the dead to bring justice to the living.

What Is Forensics?

Forensics refers to any science applied to the law. The goal of forensics is to find out how and why a person died, and who is responsible for the person's death. Several medical sciences may be forensic, such as pathology (the study of disease), toxicology (the study of drugs and poisons), serology (the study of blood and body fluids), and radiology (the study of X-rays). These forensic sciences try to answer questions such as:

- When, how, and why did the victim die?
- Was drug abuse or poisoning involved in the victim's death?
- Does the blood on the victim's clothing match blood taken from the suspect?
- Are there any weapons or foreign objects lodged inside the body, and if so what are they?

Several types of biological evidence help forensic pathologists, toxicologists, and serologists answer these questions. A corpse, skeleton, teeth, drugs, or poisons collected from the victim or suspect, stomach contents, blood and tissues, insects, and pollen samples may reveal how, where, when, and why the victim died and who is accountable for his death.

A forensic autopsy—a *postmortem* examination of a body—can reveal injuries, poisons, and other physical evidence that can place a suspect with the victim. Foreign blood and DNA collected from the victim can almost certainly accomplish the same goal. DNA and teeth can also identify an unknown victim. Plant and insect evidence not only helps link a suspect to a victim or crime scene, but also helps a forensic scientist estimate time of death, which can place a suspect with the victim at the time of the crime.

Medical sciences are particularly important to forensics because more often than not, scientific evidence decides guilt or innocence in a court case. After all, a dead body rarely lies. However, physical evidence, including trace evidence, firearms, documents, and fingerprints, provide valuable forensic clues as well. Trace evidence is any small piece of evidence that can link a suspect to a crime scene or victim. Forensic scientists examine firearms and ammunition to identify the type of weapon and match any bullets and cartridge cases found at the crime scene or inside the body to the firearm from which it was fired. Documents are useful because a hand-writing specialist can match handwriting on a document to the handwriting of a suspect. Fingerprints on bodies, murder weapons, or other objects can place the suspect at the scene of the crime.

Forensics works because everywhere a person goes, he picks up trace evidence on his shoes, clothing, skin, and hair and leaves trace evidence in each environment he visits. For example, if he takes a run in the woods behind a restaurant, walks across the red carpet in the restaurant to get a glass of water, exits the restaurant, and then goes home and walks on

A forensic autopsy may uncover clues to the manner of death.

Early Death Investigation 13

Strange but True!

Italy boasts the first medical schools in Europe, in Bologna and Padua. Before Pope Sixtus IV permitted Italian medical students to dissect human cadavers, students would often steal bodies from graves. "Body-snatching" was a common criminal activity that began in the 1300s.

Once human dissection became more popular in medical schools, body-snatching continued in other parts of Europe. In Scotland, William Burke was hanged for body-snatching in 1829 after doctors paid him and an accomplice to supply them with bodies for anatomy classes. The two men were more than grave-robbers, however. Since doctors paid less for corpses with marks on them, Burke and his accomplice developed a method of suffocation that forensic pathologists today call "burking." By sitting on the victim's chest and holding his mouth and nose closed, Burke avoided damaging the victim's body and was able to command a higher price for it. The two men killed sixteen "cadavers" before authorities caught up with them.

his blue carpet, he exchanges small items of evidence along the way. His shoes leave plant and soil material on the restaurant carpet, while picking up some of its red fibers. When he returns home, his shoes leave more plant and soil matter and red fibers from the restaurant carpet on his floor, while picking up blue fibers from his own carpet. Forensic specialists can determine the origin of the plant and soil matter and the fibers to place him in the woods behind the restaurant, in the restaurant, and in his home. Forensics is based on this sort of exchange of materials, called the Locard Exchange Principle after the police officer, Dr. Edmond Locard, who came up with the concept.

What Is Forensic Pathology?

Pathology is the study of disease, a relatively new science that began in the nineteenth century. Forensic pathology is even more recent, however, having only become a professionally recognized field in 1959.

Forensic pathology could not help solve crimes the way it does today without advances in medicine and other related sciences. One of the most important developments in forensic pathology is the autopsy. As early as

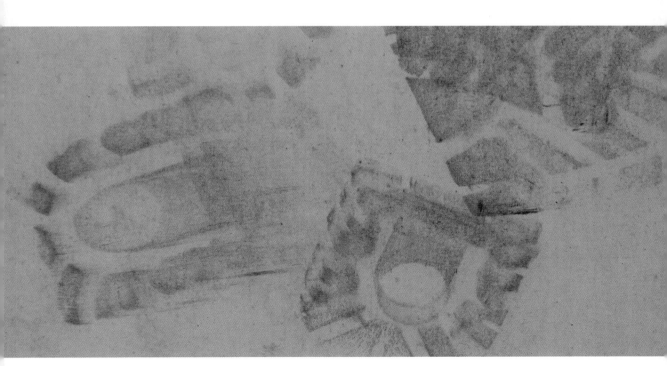

Shoe prints may carry trace evidence that places a suspect at a crime scene.

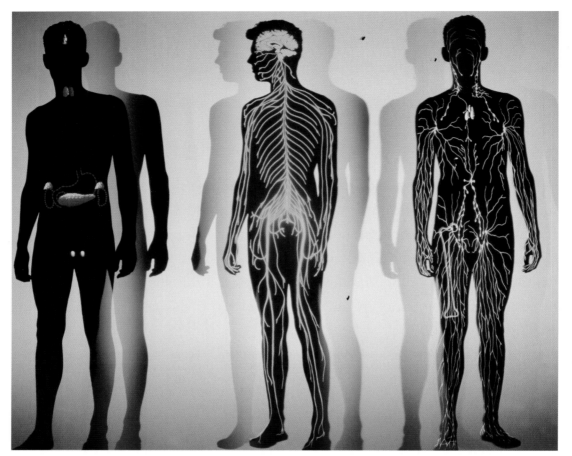

Forensic pathology uses a thorough knowledge of the human body to uncover facts about a crime.

the thirteenth century, the law department at the University of Bologna, Italy, ordered autopsies to help solve legal cases. However, even in fifteenth-century Europe, autopsies were so new and uncommon that they were often a public event. Barber-surgeons conducted autopsies and mostly examined internal organs to find out why the person died. Before the nineteenth century, autopsies were mainly the job of barber-surgeons, general physicians, the coroner, and anyone the courts could force to perform them, because pathologists did not yet exist.

Samson Ripault, a barber-surgeon, conducted the first autopsy recorded in Canada at the command of Jean-Jacques Cartier. While exploring the St. Lawrence River in 1536, a sailor collapsed and died. When Ripault investigated his body, he concluded the young man died of scurvy, a vitamin-C deficiency common among sailors. Later, during the seventeenth century, the Hôtel Dieu in Québec became the first hospital in North America. It was here that barber-surgeon Robert Gifford performed autopsies and kept meticulous records of them.

In the United States, postmortem examinations occurred as early as 1635, when a coroner in New Plymouth, New England, inspected the body of John Deacon, who he concluded to have died of "bodily weakness caused by fasting and extreme cold." In 1647, medical schools in the colonies tried to give aspiring doctors a realistic way to learn about the human body. Opening a body to observe its structure seemed the best method to train successful doctors. The General Court of Massachusetts Bay considered this argument and passed a law allowing medical students to perform an autopsy on the body of one criminal every four years.

The study of anatomy advanced more rapidly in Europe. Handbooks of human dissections, autopsy records, and illustrated guides to the human body appeared in Europe in the early 1500s, but scientists in Renaissance Italy perfected human dissection in earnest. Known as the "father of modern pathology," Giovanni Battista Morgagni of Padua published a book based on sixty years of autopsy work, De Sedibus et Causis Morborum, in 1761. He was the first scientist to describe the relationship between symptoms patients experienced before death and changes in the organs following death. Also included in his book were results of autopsies he performed, a recount of previous writings on autopsies and studies of anatomy, and the medical histories of autopsied patients.

An Austrian scientist named Carl Rokitansky was actually the first full-time pathologist in history. In his forty-five-year career, Rokitansky supervised seventy thousand autopsies and performed thirty thousand autopsies himself! Rokitansky developed a systematic method of dissecting human bodies and reporting his findings that many pathologists still use. The Rokitansky Institute where he conducted his work still stands in Vienna.

Advances in technology, beginning in the late 1600s with the invention of the microscope, allowed scientists to collect more evidence from

Giovanni Battista Morgagni

The microscope allows forensic pathologists to observe postmortem changes in body tissues.

autopsies. With microscopes, scientists could look at postmortem changes in organ tissue that could not be seen with the naked eye. By the 1800s, the development of reliable preservation methods allowed scientists to collect and store blood and tissue samples. Medical laboratories became more widespread at this time, and researchers studying human *genetics* and diseases laid the foundations of modern pathology. Today, well-equipped pathology laboratories contribute valuable scientific knowledge that helps forensic pathologists determine how and why a person died.

Early Death Investigation

Case Study: Leonardo da Vinci

Leonardo da Vinci (1452–1519), an Italian Renaissance artist and one of the world's most famous scientific geniuses, devoted much of his career to studying human anatomy. At the age of fifteen, Leonardo became an apprentice in the workshop of the well-known artist Andrea de Verrochio in Florence. It is said that the student produced works of such beauty that Verrochio could not bring himself to paint again after seeing Leonardo's creations.

The successful artist moved to Milan in 1482, where the duke commissioned his work for the next seventeen years. While in Milan, Leonardo produced studies of many subjects, including the natural world, flying machines, geometry, mechanics, and architecture. He also began studying human anatomy during this time. In fact, he spent most of his time studying science, whether observing nature or dissecting human cadavers in his workshop. He immersed himself in botany and zoology, flight, and fluid motion. Leonardo's curiosity about the way systems work led him to introduce a new method of scientific study—the systematic observation and description of subjects—which he passed on to the apprentices in his workshop.

Leonardo's workshop was not the most pleasant of places. He spent many sleepless nights dissecting corpses by candlelight, feverishly drawing and describing his observations of muscles, tendons, nerves, and joints in loose-leaf notebooks. The notebooks contained several studies of the limbs, the skin folded back to reveal intricacies of muscles and veins, and a three-dimensional sketch of the vertebrae from different perspectives. Detailed notes accompanied each of these drawings. "Frightful to behold," Leonardo remarked of the corpses lying on tables in the dim room. Working fast was a necessity, not because his subjects smelled terrible, but because refrigeration and preservatives like formaldehyde that slow down decomposition were nonexistent in sixteenth-century Italy. Da Vinci had to perform his dissections before his subjects turned to mush!

Leonardo da Vinci produced studies of thirty human cadavers during his career. Today, museums and art collectors are prepared to pay a fortune for a volume of his sketches.

Death Investigation from East to West

Forensic death investigation is an old practice dating back to thirteenth-century China. Sung Tz'u, a death investigator in a rural Chinese farming community, published a textbook called His Yuan Lu (*The Washing Away of Wrongs*) in 1250. In his handbook for students of death investigation, Sung Tz'u described postmortem examinations of human bodies, how to distinguish between injuries from sharp objects and injuries made with blunt ones, how to determine whether a person found dead in water actu-

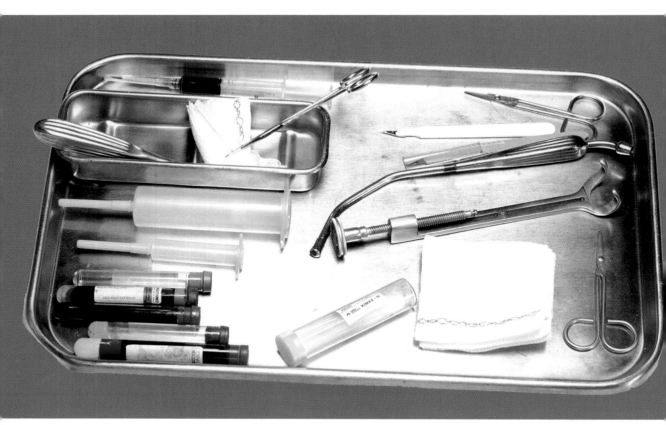

Modern tools of forensic pathology.

ally drowned or was dumped there after death, and how to distinguish between bodies burned after death and persons who actually died in fires.

The application of medicine to legal practice in Europe began as early as the fifth century, when Germanic and Slavic tribes invaded and overthrew the Roman Empire. The tribes' system of laws required a medical expert to determine the cause and manner of death in cases of foul play. According to their justice system, the perpetrator had to pay a *Wergeld*, or "blood price," to the surviving victim or his family in the case of murder. The blood price depended on the type and severity of the wounds the perpetrator inflicted and the social status of the victim. The more serious the wound, such as an injury exposing the brain or other internal organs, and the higher the class of the victim, the greater the price the perpetrator paid. For this system to work, a medical expert had to evaluate the nature and severity of the victim's wounds and report these to the courts. *The Lex Alemannorum* lists the price for different kinds of injuries in a variety of circumstances.

Nearly 800 years later, England established a coroner system in which an elected official, the coroner, was responsible for investigating suspicious and unusual deaths. The coroner's job was to examine wounds, record accusations of guilt against an individual, and arrest that individual if the wounds most likely caused the victim's death. The coroner was usually a person of wealth and status who collected a small fee for his services. He did not need any special education or qualifications and usually remained in office for life.

The first records of pathology applied to legal cases in Europe date back to 1507, when the Bamberg Code laid out a series of laws to punish criminals. In 1530, Emperor Charles V extended the code in a volume of laws called the *Consitutio Criminalis Carolina*. According to this penal code, disputes about a victim's manner of death, such as whether it was a homicide, suicide, or natural death, required court testimony from a medical expert, who would examine corpses, often by opening wounds to determine their depth and direction.

Immigrants to North America during the colonial period brought the English coroner system with them. Coroners were often corrupt, even though autopsies grew more and more common in North American death investigations. Coroners could choose to ignore autopsy results, signing the death certificate of a homicide victim as "natural." One such case took place in Maryland in 1665. Samuell Yeoungman, servant of Francis Carpenter, lay dead with multiple bruises to the head and body. A postmortem

A medical examiner must be highly qualified and able to perform medical procedures.

examination of the man's head showed two depressions in the skull and a fatal pooling of blood, most likely inflicted with a club. Francis Carpenter stood accused of beating his servant to death, but the coroner of Maryland and six lay jurors decided the young man died because he failed to see a doctor. Francis Carpenter went free.

Today in North America, the medical-examiner system of death investigation is more common than the coroner system. Under a medical-examiner system, a physician with legal training investigates suspicious, unnatural, and unusual deaths. The first medical-examiner system in the United States began in Massachusetts in 1877. In this system, a physician determined the cause and manner of death. By 1918, the medical-examiner system resembled the modern system of today. New York City designated a chief medical examiner, a physician certified in pathology, to conduct autopsies for death investigations. In Canada, provincial coroners and medical examiners investigate suspicious and unnatural deaths.

Many physicians, pathologists, and forensic scientists argue that the medical-examiner system is much more reliable than the coroner system because a coroner need not have any medical training, does not have to order an autopsy, and can decide against the results of an autopsy. In contrast, a medical examiner must be a highly qualified professional with a medical degree and specialized training in forensic pathology. The job of a medical examiner is an adventurous one when it comes to careers in crime-solving.

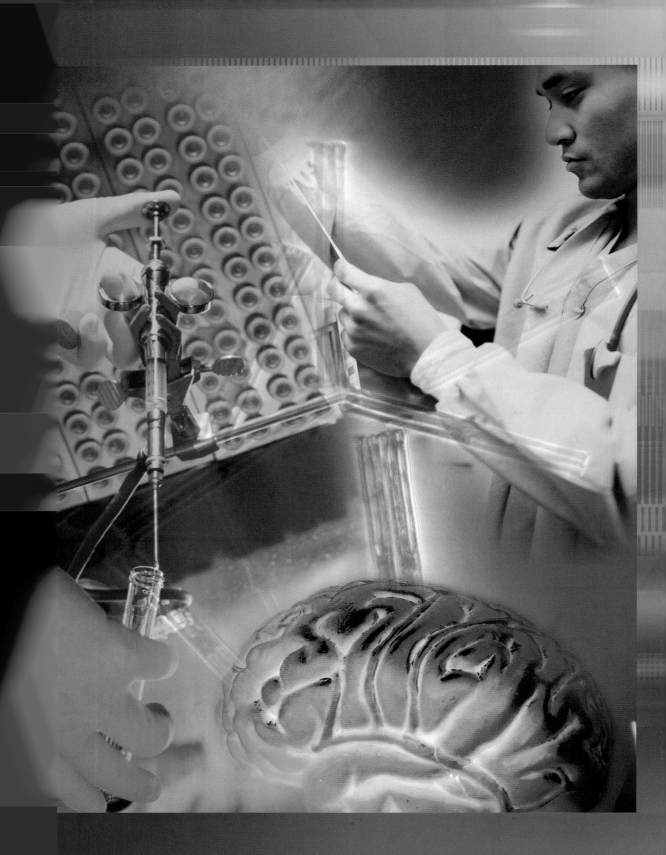

2

Forensic Pathology: Where Scientists Dare to Tread

The telephone rings. The voice of the crime-scene investigator on the other end asks the forensic pathologist to come to the crime scene, a wooded area in a rural mountain town. Pulling a jacket on, the forensic pathologist rushes out of her home in the wee hours of the morning to examine the body of a twenty-year-old woman found stabbed and half-buried under leafy debris. When she arrives at the scene, the forensic pathologist takes a camera, notebook, and pencil from the "murder bag" full of crime-scene investigation equipment in the trunk of her car and begins documenting the details of the scene: a discarded, bloody piece of clothing torn from the victim, stuck to a low tree branch; multiple bruises and cuts to the victim's face, arms, and legs; and tire treads less than a body length from where the woman lies.

Later in the morning, the conclusions the forensic pathologist will draw from her observations at the crime scene, an autopsy of the body, and other evidence from the case will have the power to put the woman's killer behind bars. A forensic pathologist is a scientist who is not afraid to tread where the dead may tell many a grim tale, if her work means keeping a community safe from danger.

Who Is the Forensic Pathologist?

A pathologist is a medical doctor who studies disease and death of the human body. When a sudden, suspicious, or accidental death occurs, a forensic pathologist is the physician who uses her medical and legal training to

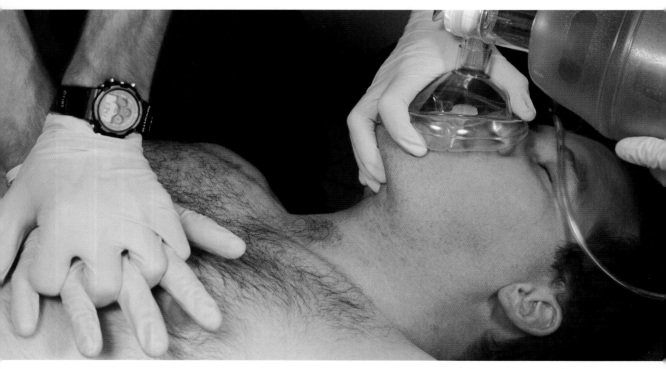

If a person arrives at the hospital unconscious (and is unable to be resuscitated), an autopsy will be performed on him.

determine when, how, and why the victim died. She also identifies unknown victims. The forensic pathologist plays a most important role in the criminal justice system because she can testify in a court of law about the circumstances surrounding a homicide, suicide, or accidental death. Her testimony is powerful because it can prove a suspect innocent or guilty of a crime.

A forensic pathologist is usually a chief or assistant medical examiner. A medical examiner investigates specific types of death that include:

- violent deaths such as homicides, suicides, and accidents
- sudden and unexpected deaths, in which the person died within hours of the appearance of symptoms or was not obviously ill
- deaths in institutions such as nursing homes, schools, and prisons
- deaths occurring during surgery or medical treatment
- deaths occurring during an abortion, no matter the legality of the procedure or who performed it
- deaths that occur within twenty-four hours of arrival at a hospital, or in situations where the deceased arrives unconscious and never regains consciousness before death
- deaths in the workplace, which usually result from violent circumstances, poisoning, or toxins in the working environment
- deaths resulting from drug or alcohol use
- deaths occurring without a physician present to confirm the circumstances surrounding the person's death
- the unexpected discovery of a body with known or unknown identity
- when the court requests the medical examiner to investigate
- any death that occurs under suspicious or unusual circumstances

In the case of some hospital deaths, a physician witnesses a patient's death, but because he finds the circumstances unusual, he contacts the medical examiner, who will determine whether the patient died of natural causes. The medical examiner decides if any of the previously described types of deaths requires an autopsy. She may decide not to perform any tests because she has concluded the death is natural, the cause of which is disease. Or she may conduct a more in-depth examination of the body, ranging from an external inspection of identifying marks and injuries to an internal examination of the organs, fluids, and tissues. The types of tests and examinations she conducts depends on the circumstances of the case.

In addition to having the power to order an autopsy, the chief medical examiner may also hire crime-scene investigators, take sworn testimony, and order the questioning of witnesses and suspects. An assistant medical examiner does not have the same authority, but helps the chief medical examiner by performing autopsies. A medical examiner may run a pathology laboratory or crime lab, and he may also investigate crime scenes and help police search for and locate bodies. Outside the laboratory, he represents the office of the chief medical examiner when he testifies in a court of law or delivers a statement to the media.

Five Critical Questions

To reconstruct the circumstances surrounding a death, the medical examiner attempts to answer five critical questions about the deceased. The importance of each question depends on the case, but hopefully the answers will lead to the perpetrator's arrest. When he investigates a death, the medical examiner asks:

- Who is the deceased?
- What is the cause of death?
- What is the mechanism of death?

- What is the manner of death?
- When did she die?

The cause of death is the factor that directly caused the victim's death, such as a bullet, poison, or run-in with the wheels of a truck. The mechanism of death is the change in the body that took place as a result of the cause of death. For example, if the cause of death is a bullet to the chest, the mechanism of death is a fatal loss of blood into the chest, loss of blood pressure, and ultimately heart failure.

The manner of death may be accidental, suicide, homicide, or natural. More than one cause or mechanism of death is possible for one manner of death. Here are some examples:

In homicide cases, the term "cause of death" refers to the murder weapon.

Forensic Pathology: Where Scientists Dare to Tread

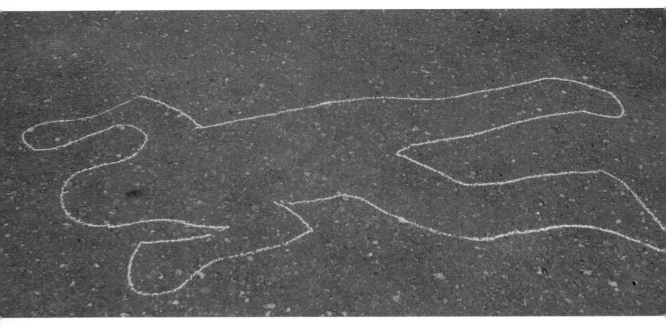

A forensic pathologist determines the manner of death.

ACCIDENTAL DEATH

A man is hard at work, fixing a fence. As he moves to step over a broken section, he trips on a loose rail and falls heavily onto his saw. The blade severs the jugular vein, which causes him to lose so much blood that his blood pressure drops and he dies of heart failure. The cause of death here is the neck wound from his saw, and the mechanism of death is the loss of blood that caused his heart to stop beating.

SUICIDAL DEATH

Another similar man is hard at work, fixing a fence. He stops cutting wood and slits his wrists with his saw, bleeding from the wounds until his blood pressure drops, eventually preventing his heart from beating. The wrist wounds from his saw caused his death, and the blood loss that stopped his heart is the mechanism of death. The manner of death is suicidal because the man inflicted the wounds himself with the intent to end his life.

HOMICIDE

Yet another man is hard at work, fixing a fence. Just as he is about to cut a new rail, an unknown attacker catches him off guard, wrestles the saw from his hand, and slits the man's throat. The man bleeds from the wound until his blood pressure drops and his heart stops. Again, the wound caused his death, and the blood loss that stopped his heart is the mechanism of death. The manner of death is homicidal because another person wounded him with the intent to kill him.

NATURAL DEATH

A fourth man is also hard at work, fixing a fence. As he cuts a plank of wood, his heart stops beating, and he falls over the side of the fence onto his saw, which cuts through his jugular vein. The cause of death is heart disease, and the mechanism of death is the weakening of the heart muscle that eventually caused his heart to stop beating. The manner of death is natural because a disease caused his death before he fell on the saw.

Sometimes forensic pathologists disagree among themselves about the manner of death, and sometimes the manner of death the medical examiner decides on changes as new information comes to light. Based on crime-scene evidence, a death may appear suicidal, but the medical examiner will most likely wait to assemble the entire body of evidence before he issues his final opinion. New evidence could suggest a murder rather than a suicide, as was the case in Lonnie Ted Binion's untimely death (see case study on page 34).

Case Study:
Lonnie Ted Binion

On September 17, 1998, paramedics found Lonnie Ted Binion dead in his Las Vegas home. An empty bottle of Xanax, an addictive prescription drug, lay next to the wealthy casino executive. This, combined with a hysterical interview with Binion's girlfriend, Sandy Murphy, led police to believe Binion died of a drug overdose. However, Binion's autopsy and other evidence in the case later suggested otherwise.

With the help of a private investigator, new evidence came to light. Binion had buried a large cache of silver worth about seven million dollars in the Las Vegas desert. After his death, police arrested a man named Rick Tabish for digging up and stealing the silver. As it turned out, Tabish was Sandy Murphy's lover, and was deeply in debt. Binion's autopsy revealed a large amount of Xanax in his tissues, and when the medical examiner listed the cause of death as a suicidal drug overdose, Binion's family asked a consulting forensic pathologist for a second opinion.

What the consulting forensic pathologist saw in his review of reports and photographs from the crime scene and the autopsy led him to a completely different conclusion from that of the medical examiner. Hemorrhages in the eyes suggested someone had suffocated Binion. The forensic pathologist also noticed what might have been handcuff marks on Binion's wrist, marks on his chest that looked like the buttons of his shirt had been pressed into his skin with some force, and linear abrasions around his lips. The evidence pointed to a method of suffocation called burking. If this cause of death were true, it would suggest Sandy Murphy had staged the crime scene to look like Ted Binion committed suicide.

On May 19, 2000, after hearing both the medical examiner's and the consulting forensic pathologist's expert testimony, a jury convicted Murphy and Tabish of first-degree murder.

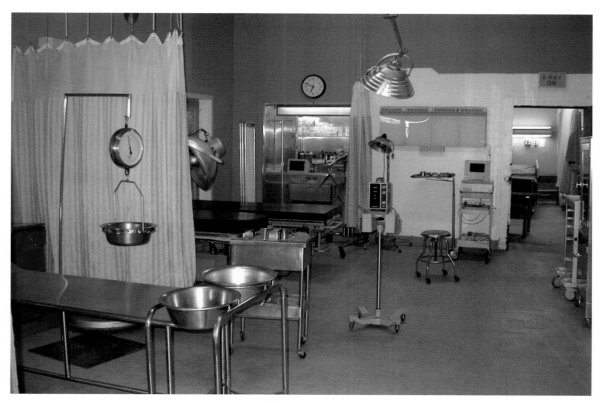

A morgue

THE MEDICAL EXAMINER'S OFFICE

Medical examiners work in a regional, state, territory, or provincial medical-examiner system. This type of system includes the chief medical examiner, the assistant medical examiner(s), and laboratory and office staff who work in the office of the chief medical examiner. The office of the chief medical examiner is usually located in the state capital. The office has a well-equipped forensics laboratory for investigating physical evidence and a morgue for storing and examining bodies.

In the United States, sixteen states have a state medical-examiner system. Seven more have a county by county medical-examiner system, eleven have a county coroner system, and the rest have a mixed system. A coroner's powers are similar to those of a chief medical examiner, but unlike a medical examiner, he can be held personally responsible for any mistakes he makes when investigating a suspicious death.

DEDICATION, ETHICS, AND INTEGRITY

A medical examiner's job is demanding to say the least. He may perform as many as 250 autopsies each year, and in addition to his medical work, he testifies in several trials. A medical examiner's conclusions are not always popular with the general public, so he must also withstand criticism from individuals as well as the media. In a court of law, lawyers may question his scientific methods or even his educational and career background to make sure his conclusions about when, how, and why a person died are more than likely accurate. Additionally, lawyers may attempt to discredit his findings and opinions by asking him questions about his personal life. This sort of interrogation makes most scientists uncomfortable. A forensic pathologist must be a well-trained, experienced scientist with strong ethics and self-confidence to successfully manage this sort of scrutiny.

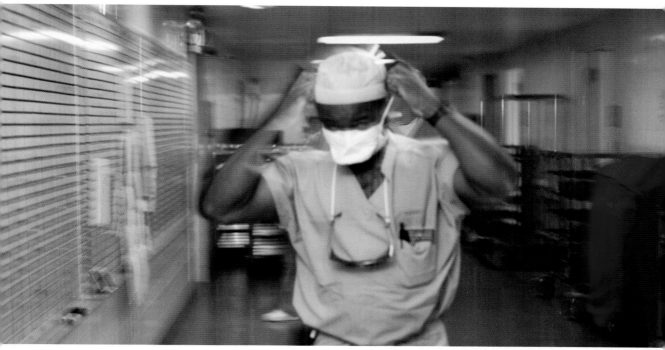

A forensic pathologist must complete four years of medical school.

The Model Post-mortem Examinations Act of 1954 lays down the responsibilities and desired qualities of the chief medical examiner. Section three of the act reads, "It is basic to any properly organized *medico-legal* investigative system that the head of the Office be a person of the highest mental and moral caliber, with the best obtainable professional training in medicine and pathology."

A forensic pathologist must have strong ethics and personal integrity because the search for truth is at the heart of her job. She must be able to investigate a death without letting her own biases or those of anyone else influence her conclusions. For example, a family might ask the forensic

Case Study:
Meet the Forensic Pathologist

Dr. Michael Baden, forensic pathologist and coauthor of two books, *Dead Reckoning: The New Science of Catching Killers* and *Unnatural Death: Confessions of a Medical Examiner*, has gained international recognition as one of the leading forensic pathologists in the United States. Dr. Baden is one of just three hundred full-time forensic pathologists in the country. Having performed over 20,000 autopsies since he began work as New York City's medical examiner in 1960, Dr. Baden interprets the subtleties of wounds and bruises to solve a variety of crimes.

When someone dies in a traffic accident, in prison, or in the custody of the police, Dr. Baden gets involved. He works with the living as well as victims who have long been dead. In rape and abuse cases, Dr. Baden examines cuts, bruises, gunshot wounds, and trace evidence on living victims to find out how the crime happened and who committed it. When new information about an old case comes to light, Dr. Baden helps exhume and re-examine a victim's remains, which are usually no more than bones.

He has been an investigator and expert witness in several notorious homicide cases, such as those involving JonBenet Ramsey, Nicole Brown Simpson, and Ted Binion. Dr. Baden has also brought his expertise to the Forensic Pathology Panel of the U.S. Congress

Select Committee on Assassinations, where he helped investigate the assassinations of President John F. Kennedy, Dr. Martin Luther King Jr., and Medgar Evers. In 1992, he traveled to Russia to work on a forensics team whose task was to determine whether a mass burial of bones belonged to Tsar Nicholas II and the royal Romanov family, whom Bolsheviks murdered during World War I.

Dr. Baden now works as the codirector of the Medico-legal Investigative Unit of the New York State Police, so he is "on call," or ready to conduct autopsies, analyze evidence, and consult with law enforcement and victims twenty-four hours a day, seven days a week. Additionally, Dr. Baden is a visiting professor at New York Law School, Albert Einstein School of Medicine, John Jay College of Criminal Justice, and Albany Medical Center.

pathologist to change her conclusion about how their loved one died. The family might not want the general public to know their loved one committed suicide. Similarly, certain officials might not want the general public to know that a respected politician committed a grizzly murder, so they might pressure the forensic pathologist not to testify in court. It is the responsibility of the forensic pathologist to present scientific facts regardless of the consequences. She is the voice of those who can no longer speak for themselves.

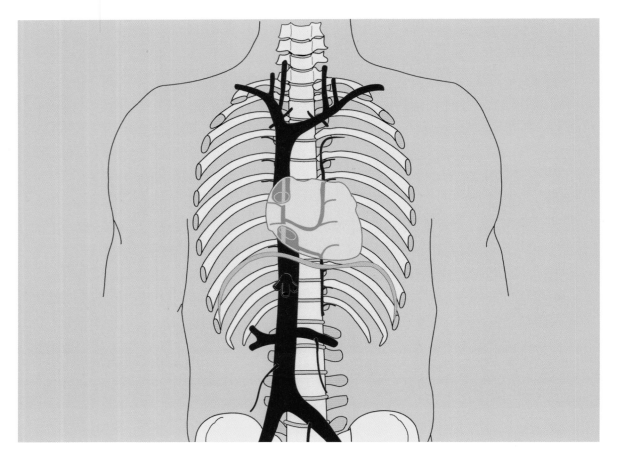

The forensic pathologist must be highly knowledgeable about human anatomy.

So You Want to Be a Forensic Pathologist?

Becoming a forensic pathologist requires many years of training. To reconstruct the circumstances surrounding a mysterious death, a forensic pathologist must have expert knowledge of human anatomy, pathology, anthropology, laboratory analysis such as microscopy and X-ray testing, procedures for collecting evidence, investigating crime scenes, and giving expert testimony, as well as federal, state, and local laws. Someone who wants to become a forensic pathologist must complete four years of college or university study, four years of medical school, a three- to five-year training program in pathology, and a year-long training program in forensic pathology. That adds up to about fourteen years of school! After completing her education, a pathologist must pass an exam that certifies she has the appropriate training to embark on a successful career. The American Board of Pathology designs this exam and issues certificates to those who pass.

A forensic pathologist must have more than medico-legal training to become a medical examiner, however. He must also have expert knowledge of engineering, police science, criminology, political science, and criminalistics. And, although he is a trained scientist, this does not mean that he need not be creative. On the contrary, many fields of science like medicine, chemistry, and physics require thinking "outside the box," and forensic pathology is no exception. A forensic pathologist must be an excellent problem-solver who can consider numerous possible solutions to a problem.

A forensic pathologist works closely with a variety of people: crime-scene investigators and technicians; other forensic pathologists and physicians; forensic toxicologists, entomologists, odontologists, and anthropologists; firearms and ballistics experts; fingerprint, footprint, and DNA specialists; and hair, fiber, and trace evidence scientists. These are just some of the forensic professionals with whom a forensic pathologist needs to collaborate to solve a case. Beyond the laboratory, she may interact with family members of the deceased, members of the media, and lawyers, judges, and juries in a court of law.

Excellent communication skills are a must because a forensic pathologist needs to discuss a case with both scientists and laypeople to provide the most accurate information possible about the circumstances of a person's

Great Forensic Scientists:
The Vidocq Society

The Vidocq Society is a group of forensic scientists (including forensic pathologists, anthropologists, and psychologists) and law enforcement agents who devote their spare time to investigating unsolved deaths. By putting many heads together, the commission has helped close the lid on many criminal cases.

These professionals named the society after Eugene François Vidocq, whose values they admire. An unconventional detective in early nineteenth-century Paris, Vidocq devoted his life to capturing the guilty and freeing the innocent. Among his many achievements, Vidocq was the first detective to make plaster-of-paris casts of shoe prints and footprints, as well as the first to use ballistics and criminalistics to solve crimes. He established a modern detective agency and made a career of scouring Paris streets in search of criminals. Sir Arthur Conan Doyle is said to have based the character of Sherlock Holmes on Vidocq.

death. When talking to other physicians or forensic pathologists, he uses very specific scientific language to convey information. If he has a concern with which he needs help, a detailed question will allow another physician or forensic pathologist to give a more precise answer. A question a forensic pathologist might ask is: "Would you agree the *subdural* hematoma (blood clot) was the contributing cause of death?" Physicians will understand this medical language, but non-scientists most likely will not.

Many cases go to trial, and therefore a forensic pathologist often testifies as an expert witness. An expert witness is a professional who has many years of experience in her field of work and can provide detailed, in-depth information about certain kinds of evidence. She is the only kind of witness who can present a conclusion or opinion about the evidence, and a lawyer may ask her to testify against the conclusions of another scientist. In a trial, a forensic pathologist must present the conclusions of her autopsy report in language that nonscientists can easily understand. Her job is important because she helps the jury weigh the evidence against the defendant. But if the evidence consists of too much *scientific jargon*—the language only scientists use—the jury may not understand it well enough to make an accurate decision about the defendant's guilt or innocence. A term like "subdural hematoma" might leave a jury full of blank faces.

A difficult aspect of a forensic pathologist's job is collecting information about the victim from the family while being sensitive to their loss. He might want to find out about the victim's personal history, such as where she worked, what hobbies interested her, and how her emotional health appeared. Or he might be present when the family identifies the body at the morgue facility near his office. The role of a forensic pathologist in this situation is similar to that of a physician, because not only does he discuss the circumstances of the victim's death with the family, but he also gives them emotional support in their time of grief.

Most forensic pathologists love their jobs because they can use their medical and legal training to bring justice and help protect their community. A forensic pathologist is a person who is naturally curious and enthusiastic about forensic science. Her career is exciting and adventurous because she never knows what kind of case will be waiting for her when she arrives at her office. Sometimes, the real adventure begins in the dark hours of the morning when she receives a call to examine a crime scene.

Forensic Pathology: Where Scientists Dare to Tread

3

The Crime Scene

When Nicole Brown Simpson and Ronald Goldman were murdered outside her home on June 12, 1994, O. J. Simpson, Nicole's former husband, became the primary suspect. Crime-scene investigators examined the scene, but because they handled the victims' bodies carelessly and failed to protect evidence from contamination when they collected it, valuable evidence was lost. Based on the handling of the evidence, a jury acquitted Simpson of the murders.

Evidence collection at a crime scene is one of the most important aspects of crime-solving. The O. J. Simpson case is a sobering example of how overlooked clues and damaged evidence can negatively impact a criminal investigation. In fact, this case increased public awareness of the importance of the investigation procedure at a crime scene. Details of evidence collection and handling were subject to acute criticism from the general public over the course of the high-profile trial, more so than in any other criminal case in history.

A forensic pathologist, a coroner, a crime-scene investigator, or a detective may all investigate and collect evidence at a crime scene, but if they do not protect the evidence, the forensic pathologist may only be able to draw limited conclusions from his examination of the body when it arrives at his office. To reconstruct the chain of events leading up to a crime, investigators must avoid disturbing the crime scene in any way. For this reason, forensic pathologists often give lectures and other educational classes to law enforcement personnel about how to protect and collect evidence on or near a body. When a forensic pathologist responds to a crime scene, he follows a step-by-step procedure to make sure all of the important evidence arrives at his office intact.

Arriving at the Scene

When a death investigator such as a medical examiner, coroner, or specially trained detective arrives at a crime scene, she first makes sure the scene is safe to enter by looking for hazards such as unstable structures, fire, poisonous gases, and hostile crowds. If the scene is safe, she puts on gear that protects her from dangerous biological and chemical substances and also protects the crime scene from contamination. For example, she covers her head with a plastic cap to keep her hair from falling onto surfaces at the scene and wears paper booties over her shoes so she will not track in foreign materials such as fibers, soil, and dust. Latex gloves prevent her from leaving fingerprints on the body and other evidence. Imagine the confusion a stray hair from the medical examiner's head would cause if it fell on the clothing of the victim and later ended up under analysis at the forensics laboratory!

After she suits up, the medical examiner introduces herself to other officials and staff at the scene. These people may include police officers, paramedics, and social or child protective services, as well as forensic entomologists and photographers. Together they will make a plan of action so they can investigate the scene in an organized way without overlooking or losing valuable evidence. The first person to arrive at the scene has set up a barrier around the area to prevent passers-by from entering and contaminating the scene. She may also cover the body with a clean white sheet to shield it from view if it is in a public area.

At the crime scene, examiners will look for clues.

The Crime Scene   **47**

A crime-scene photographer records evidence.

The medical examiner observes the entire scene before examining the body or collecting evidence. Most important, her survey of the scene helps her find the location of the body. If she finds the body merely consists of bones, she will know to consult a forensic anthropologist, a scientist who specializes in examining bones, and a forensic odontologist, a scientist who studies teeth, to determine the identity of the victim and any injuries he may have sustained. Walking through the crime scene helps her find fragile evidence she or a professional crime-scene photographer must immediately photograph and that the crime scene investigator must then collect. A "walk-through" helps her decide what sort of investigation to carry out as well. She will look closely for different kinds of clues if she suspects foul play, and she will need different types of tools to collect the evidence. For this reason, the medical examiner must be ready for any scenario.

Forensic Pathologists Are Always Prepared

Medical examiners must be prepared for a call to a crime scene on very short notice. Should he need to visit a crime scene right away, a medical examiner keeps a crime scene bag, or one or two large toolboxes full of the equipment he uses to investigate a crime scene, in his car. Under exceptional circumstances, such as when the crime scene is unusually far away from law enforcement and medical facilities, he may need to conduct an internal examination of the body right at the crime scene.

When she walks through a crime scene for the first time, the medical examiner or a professional photographer documents evidence in the condition she found it—the location and features of the site; the position and condition of the body which may be buried, half-covered in

What's in the Bag?

Some equipment in a forensic pathologist's portable "murder bag," or toolbox might be:

1. investigative notebook and pencil for recording crime-scene notes
2. cellular telephone, radio, and pager for communicating with other officials
3. waterproof apron and rubber gloves
4. disposable paper overalls, hair cover, shoe covers, and face mask
5. boots and raincoat
6. thermometer for taking body temperature
7. syringes, needles, and sterile swabs for collecting blood, body fluids, and other evidence from the body
8. autopsy dissection kit with a handsaw for cutting through bone
9. needles and twine to close incisions in the body
10. swabs and containers for sampling blood and body fluids
11. preservative jars to protect tissue samples
12. inventory lists to keep track of evidence
13. body charts for recording external injuries
14. trace evidence kit
15. blood test kit
16. latent fingerprint kit

17. gunshot residue kit
18. rape kit
19. body ID tags and body bags
20. bags to cover the victim's hands and feet
21. hand-held microscopic lens
22. tool kit (measuring tape, shovel, screwdriver, hammer, bolt cutters)
23. electric flashlight for working at night
24. mini tape recorder for recording observations
25. digital camera and/or video camera for documenting external injuries, the position of the body in relation to objects nearby, and other details of the crime scene

debris, submerged in water, or fully exposed to the elements; injuries to the body; the location of the murder weapon in relation to other objects at the scene; or the features of and damages to the vehicle in the case of an accident or abduction. A digital or video camera is an important piece of equipment for reviewing the scene later. Often, a fresh pair of eyes can pick out important details that might have been overlooked the day before. For example, the scene of a rape-homicide may at first yield no clues as to the perpetrator, but when a forensic pathologist reviews photographs and video footage of the scene the following day, she might notice a small semen stain on a patch of leaves near the body. This could eventually lead investigators to the perpetrator because semen contains

DNA. If a suspect's DNA does not match that extracted from the semen, he is almost certainly not the perpetrator.

Forensic pathologists in the United States and Canada rarely visit a crime scene, however, and usually perform autopsies at special morgue facilities in the building where they work. But in more remote states, provinces, and territories, and in developing countries where crime-scene investigation teams are small or nonexistent, forensic pathologists may routinely collect crime-scene evidence.

Processing the Scene

After the medical examiner and other crime-scene investigators survey the scene, they begin "processing" evidence, or collecting clues. This may involve gathering trace evidence such as hairs, fibers, fingerprints, and dust from the interior of a car or the victim's clothes; collecting soil and insect specimens on or near the body; and placing murder weapons, personal effects, and other material evidence—anything from newspapers to ham-and-cheese sandwiches—into plastic evidence bags with labels that record the date, time, and location where the investigator found the evidence. The evidence depends on the nature of the case.

The medical examiner must maintain a chain-of-custody record for all evidence collected at the crime scene. A chain-of-custody record lists the name of each person who handled the evidence and the departments in the forensics laboratory in which the sample has been. For example, he may draw a vial of blood from the victim of a fatal car accident right at the crime scene if the victim is recently deceased. The blood will be easier to collect because it will be more fluid at this time. The medical examiner will then send the sample to the toxicology department of his forensics laboratory, where specialists will test the blood for alcohol and other drugs,

Collecting DNA

In 2002, a woman was found murdered in her home in Martha's Vineyard, Massachusetts. It appeared as though she had been raped, and she had died of a stab wound. Her two-and-a-half-year-old daughter sat next to her.

Although many people were interviewed, investigators hit a wall in finding her killer. The woman's family even offered a reward, but law enforcement seemed no nearer to finding the killer.

In 2005, stymied investigators asked male residents to submit to DNA testing. Many complied; others did not. Civil liberties groups went to court to try and stop the testing.

In April of 2005, a man was arrested for the woman's murder. Because he was acquainted with the victim and had a history of violence against women, investigators had asked him for a DNA sample—in 2004, the year before the mass testing. A backlog in the Massachusetts laboratory had delayed processing the test—and finding the alleged killer—for a year.

a routine test in the case of vehicle accidents. The toxicologist will sign the chain-of-custody record.

Removing the Body

Once the medical examiner locates the body, she checks for a pulse, breathing, and reflexes to make sure the victim is dead. Her official pronounce-

Spotlight on the Medical Examiner's Sidekick: The Forensic Investigator

The medical examiner's job is so busy that having a sidekick—a forensic specialist to help with all of his duties—is a necessity. At the crime scene and at the morgue, the forensic investigator represents the medical examiner's office and works beside the medical examiner herself. The forensic investigator may take legal responsibility for the body at the crime scene, perform a general examination of the body at the scene, collect trace evidence and insects from the body, take the liver temperature of the body to help estimate the victim's time of death, wrap the body, and transport it from the crime scene to the medical examiner's office.

At the medical examiner's office, the forensic investigator helps with nearly every part of the medical examiner's job by assisting or conducting autopsies; writing autopsy reports under the medical examiner's supervision; explaining autopsy results to family and friends of the victim; speaking to the public, the media, and law enforcement; and testifying in the medical examiner's place in a court of law.

ment of death places the body under the jurisdiction of the medical examiner's or coroner's office. She takes the rectal temperature of the body with a thermometer and records the air temperature at the crime scene to help estimate the victim's time of death. If she suspects a rape occurred, she may collect blood and semen specimens at the crime scene. She or a forensic entomologist may collect insects from the body and the soil around and underneath it. A forensic palynologist—a scientist who uses pollen evidence to solve crimes—may collect pollen from the hair, skin, and clothing of the victim and from the soil around or under the victim. The medical examiner takes any personal effects from the scene, including identification cards, wallets, purses, and discarded clothing, and places these in separate evidence bags with special evidence labels. Next, she gives the body an identification tag and places bags over the hands and feet to prevent trace evidence, such as blood or skin cells under the fingernails, from being lost. She then zips the body into a black plastic body bag that protects it from contamination on its way from the crime scene to her office.

In most cases, the medical examiner must examine the body at his office to determine the identity of the victim and the cause, manner, mechanism, and time of death. Once the body arrives at the office, the medical examiner can begin examining it to tease out the story of the victim's death.

4

Examining the Body

The infamous serial killer Ted Bundy is thought to have murdered as many as forty to fifty young women over a period of less than ten years. He began killing in 1969, moving from California to Oregon, Washington, and Utah before police finally apprehended him.

One fateful night in Salt Lake City in 1974, Bundy abducted and attempted to attack Carol DaRonch, who luckily escaped and identified him in a police lineup. Bundy was sentenced to fifteen years in prison, but he escaped twice, the second time eluding police long enough to go on another killing spree.

In 1978, Bundy attacked four young women at Florida State University, killing two and injuring two others. Police later caught up with him, but not because he failed to cover his tracks. On the contrary, Bundy managed to kill again, taking the life of a twelve-year-old girl. Not too long after the murder, policed stopped him for driving under the influence. Bundy was later tried for the murders of the Florida State University students, but he pleaded not guilty.

Expert testimony from a forensic pathologist helped convict Ted Bundy of the murders. The autopsy of one of the young women showed a bite mark on the left buttock. The photographer attending the autopsy took a photograph of the bite and the forensic pathologist measured it. When the forensic pathologist compared the bite mark with photographs and a cast of Bundy's teeth, it was almost certain that Bundy had bitten the victim.

On the basis of this evidence, the jury convicted Ted Bundy of murder. He was executed ten years later, in 1989.

The forensic pathologist noticed the bite mark that helped convict Ted Bundy of murder during an external examination of the victim. When a forensic pathologist, often the medical examiner, looks at a body for the first time in the morgue, he examines the body from the outside in. How extensive an examination he does is his decision and depends on the circumstances of the case.

Choosing the Right Autopsy

Most of the excitement in a forensic pathologist's day takes place in the morgue—a sterile room lined with steel examination tables and large, refrigerated coolers that store bodies waiting to be examined. When the medical examiner's office agrees to take responsibility for a body, the body arrives at the morgue in a black, plastic body bag. Technicians place an ID label with the person's name outside the bag to help them find the body among up to seventy-five others in the cooler. The body stays in the cooler until the forensic pathologist and her team of technicians performs an autopsy.

The chief medical examiner (forensic pathologist) performs the autopsy in a way that will provide the needed answers, so what she examines depends on the details of the case. When she arrives at work each morning, the first thing she does is look at a list of bodies delivered to the morgue. Each body will have a death-scene investigative report, a police report, medical records, and other evidence such as receipts, a piece of personal mail, or a wallet and keys. The forensic pathologist reviews all of this information to decide what sort of exam to do. No matter what kind of autopsy she chooses, the goal of the autopsy is always the same: to determine the mechanism, cause, manner, and time of death, and, in some cases, the identity of the deceased. In the process, she works closely with many other forensic scientists and laboratory departments, including forensic toxicologists; chemists; serologists; immunologists; anthropologists; photographers;

entomologists; the departments of fire arms and ballistics; and professionals that analyze hair, fibers, and trace evidence, and fingerprint, footprint, and DNA evidence.

He will choose the exam method from three types of autopsies: external, partial, and internal. If the cause and manner of death are obvious from the way the body looks, he performs an external exam. An external autopsy is an examination of the entire outside of the body. The forensic pathologist looks for scars, preexisting or postmortem injuries, trauma, trace evidence, and any postmortem changes in the appearance of the body.

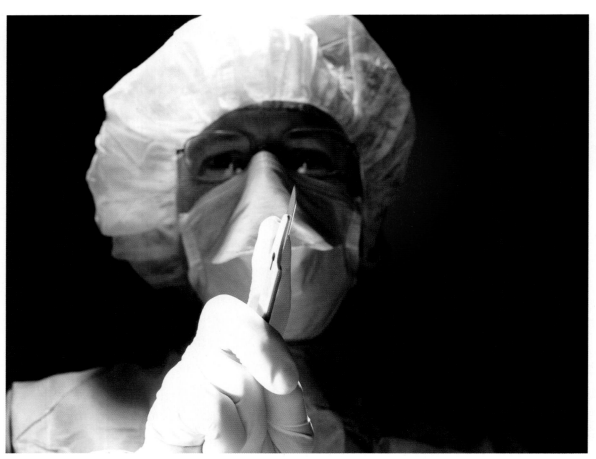

A medical examiner will perform an external, partial, or internal autopsy.

Case Study:
Buried Alive?

A dead body is the most important requirement for an autopsy. This may seem like an obvious fact, but four hundred years ago being buried alive was a legitimate fear. When science was in its early stages, accurately confirming death eluded many physicians. In fact, discerning whether a person was actually dead was such a matter of guesswork that a weak heartbeat was all one needed to be pronounced "dead." The stethoscope had not yet been invented, so death investigators felt or listened for a heartbeat, a method that is most unreliable. In the 1600s, a new technique somewhat alleviated these fears, though it was nearly just as disconcerting. Family members sat in waiting mortuaries watching those presumed dead. A person with cold, clammy skin who was weak and unresponsive could have appeared dead, yet really have been alive but gravely ill. Only when a body began to decay was the person pronounced dead and prepared for burial.

Today, fairly recent technology makes determining death more accurate. The electrocardiogram (EKG) records the electrical energy of the beating heart, so the absence of a detectable electrical current helps doctors confirm death.

Many morgues boast a portion of a Latin proverb, "Hic locus est ubi mors gaudet succurrere vitae," on a door or wall. The phrase means, "This is the place where death delights to help the living." Indeed, forensic pathologists devote their careers to recovering truth and justice from the silent testimony of the dead.

If the cause and manner of death are not initially apparent, the forensic pathologist performs a partial autopsy. A partial autopsy is an external exam followed by a detailed examination of one area of the body. The forensic pathologist may look closely at the brain for signs of a blood clot, he may examine the chest area to determine whether the deceased had heart disease, or he may investigate the abdominal cavity for signs of kidney, liver, or intestinal irregularities.

An internal examination is a thorough, step-by-step investigation of all the organs, tissues, and fluids in the body. The forensic pathologist looks for internal evidence of recent or preexisting disease, trauma, and injuries, and for changes in the appearance of the body caused by natural decomposition.

Beginning the Examination

The forensic pathologist puts on her white smock and latex gloves. After reviewing all the facts surrounding the death, she has decided to do an internal autopsy. An autopsy technician removes the body from the cooler. Together, the forensic pathologist and the technician, or assisting forensic pathologist in a medical examiner's office, remove the body from the body bag, weigh the body, measure its height, and place it on an examination table. The forensic pathologist notes the sex, eye color, and hair color and takes fingerprints and footprints from the body. A photographer takes a photograph of the face to identify the body after the exam and a photograph of the entire body that documents the condition in which it arrived at the morgue.

The forensic pathologist begins the autopsy with an external examination, recording her observations of the type and condition of the person's clothing, jewelry, and any other items the person may have been wearing when he died. After these items are removed, another photograph is taken of the body to record its condition before the autopsy. This photograph will document any scars, injuries, or signs of trauma the forensic pathologist notes in the external examination, and will be important evidence if an investigator calls on the pathologist to testify in a court of law. The forensic pathologist wraps the person's clothes, jewelry, and other personal possessions in white paper to protect any trace evidence that might be on them, such as dust, fibers, and fingerprints. She records the size and brand of the clothing and jewelry and sends these items to the forensics laboratory, where forensic pathology technicians examine them for trace evidence.

The forensic pathologist thoroughly investigates the outside of the body, noting any scars, evidence of old or recent trauma, injuries, natural disease, and any irregularities. Also noted are identifying characteristics such as tattoos and piercings that may help her find out who the person is. She collects any foreign objects or materials from the eyes, nose, mouth, and vagina, and from under the fingernails. She also looks for broken fingernails. If a person fought his attacker, the forensic pathologist will find the perpetrator's skin cells under the victim's fingernails. DNA extracted from these skin cells can help reveal the identity of the killer.

She will also read the notes taken by the medical examiner at the crime scene. He will have collected any insects from openings in the body such as the mouth, nose, eyes, and ears, and from wounds. The medical examiner will also have noted evidence of decomposition and will have flexed the limbs to determine the degree of rigor mortis—the stiffening of muscles following death. Taking the temperature of the body is an important part of the medical examiner's exam because the forensic pathologist can use this information to make a rough estimate of the person's time of death. At the end of the exam, she may X-ray the body to look for broken or fractured bones.

When she finds an important clue, the forensic pathologist records her observations on an autopsy chart—a sheet of paper with a systematic autopsy **protocol** from external to internal examination and a diagram of the human body on which she can make notes. The forensic pathologist will record the mechanism, cause, and manner of death on this form, and the facts supporting her conclusions.

Trace Evidence

The medical examiner collects trace evidence from the outside of the body. She combs the victim's head and pubic hair to dislodge pollen, soil, foreign hairs, fibers, and other evidence. She takes head, eyebrow, and pubic hair samples from the victim to compare with foreign hair samples collected from the victim or elsewhere at the crime scene.

Different lighting techniques reveal trace evidence such as hair, fibers, pollen, blood, saliva, semen, and fingerprints the medical examiner would not otherwise be able to see. When lasers or ultraviolet light reveal such evidence, the medical examiner collects it and sends it to the forensics lab for analysis.

Injuries

When the medical examiner inspects the outside of the body, he looks for injuries such as cuts, bruises, bite marks, and needle pricks. During his examination, he is trying to find out the type, distribution, pattern, cause, and direction of injuries; which injuries are major or minor, old, recent, or postmortem; how the injuries occurred; and what produced them.

Injuries may be penetrating or nonpenetrating. Penetrating injuries, such as those from bullets, knives, and bombs, are injuries that pierce the skin. They may consist of entrance as well as exit wounds. The medical examiner looks for evidence of gunpowder, singed hair, and burns around gunshot wounds. The presence or absence of these markings helps determine the distance between the gun and the victim at the time the gun went off. He locates the entry wound, which is typically small and clean, and the exit

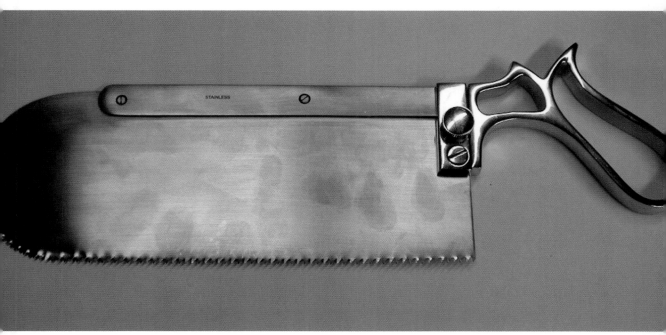

A bone saw may be used during an autopsy.

Case Study: The Green River Killer

On a sunny day in August of 1982, Robert Ainsworth took his raft to the Green River for a day of fishing. Later that day, he spoke briefly with a man standing on the riverbank, and then continued drifting downriver in search of more fish. What he soon discovered in the water were not fish but human bodies.

Shocked, Ainsworth reached out to grab the hand of a half-clothed woman, floating in the water near his raft. He fell into the water before he could reach her, and as he made his way to land, he discovered the body of another woman, also half-clothed. When detectives arrived soon after his discovery, the body of a sixteen-year-old girl turned up in a field not far from the river.

From the autopsies, medical examiner Dr. Donald Reay concluded the cause of death was strangulation, the manner homicide. The perpetrator had dumped the two bodies in the river after killing them. One body found in the river was in an advanced state of decomposition. The body of the sixteen-year-old girl had bruises on her arms and legs that indicated she might have fought her attacker before she died. Dr. Reay collected semen samples from the women that indicated the perpetrator raped them before he killed them.

Over the next six months, detectives would discover a total of six bodies at the Green River site. However, the primary suspect, Gary Leon Ridgway, went free. Nearly twenty years later, after the development of DNA technology, DNA extracted from the semen samples Dr. Reay had collected matched DNA taken from Ridgway when investigators first opened the case. Police arrested Ridgway on four counts of aggravated murder.

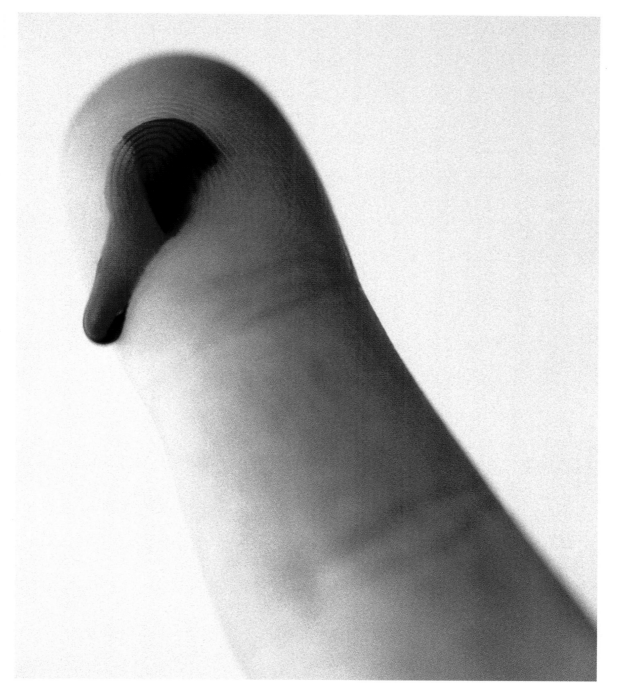

A penetrating injury pierces the skin.

Case Study:
Debunking a Conspiracy Theory

President John F. Kennedy was assassinated in 1963 during a parade in Dallas, Texas. Commander James J. Humes conducted Kennedy's autopsy at Bethesda Naval Hospital in Washington, D.C., but this was his first case involving a gunshot wound. Unfortunately, he did not conduct a full autopsy, following instructions only to find the bullet, which authorities believed was still in the body. He never turned the body over or called the Dallas hospital where Kennedy had been taken. Had Dr. Humes done so, he would have learned doctors there had performed a surgical procedure going through an exit wound in the president's neck. He never shaved the head to examine the wound more clearly, and the wound was photographed through hair. The doctor also miscalculated the wound's location by four inches. He then burned the notes he made during the autopsy because they were covered in blood, and later rewrote his notes from memory, mistakenly adding observations he had never made. Included in these notes was a disastrous assumption that the bullet entered and exited the same wound in Kennedy's head. Even worse, he could not determine how many shots had been fired.

Kennedy's assassination remained a mystery for fifteen years, until a team of forensic pathologists, led by renowned forensic pathologist Dr. Michael Baden, exhumed Kennedy's body. They reviewed autopsy reports and photographs, X-rays, crime-scene photographs, and Kennedy's clothing. It was the bullet holes in the clothing that led them to conclude that two bullets, not one, had hit Kennedy from behind: one entering his throat and wounding Governor Connally, who sat in front of him in the car, and the second entering the back of his head and landing in the front of the car.

Among the team's recommendations after the examination was the need for national attention to be paid to improving death investigation. The original autopsy was incomplete and performed by an unqualified doctor, resulting in misleading conclusions. According to Dr. Baden, in the hands of a hospital pathologist, "Those doctors made a lot of mistakes, such as creating false descriptions for why they couldn't find the bullet. They said it and they were wrong, and it lives with us still."

wound, which is larger and not as neat. The medical examiner may make a cast of a knife wound to estimate the shape and size of the weapon. Or he may be able to describe the weapon based on the marks the handle of the knife leaves imprinted on the skin. He will measure the depth and direction of any sharp-force injuries—injuries from sharp weapons. If he finds needle pricks to the skin, he will be sure to send a blood sample to the lab for a drug test because needle pricks suggest the victim abused drugs.

X-rays of the body reveal foreign objects such as a knife blade or a bullet that may remain inside a wound and broken bones that may have resulted from a gunshot wound. An X-ray can show the path a bullet traveled

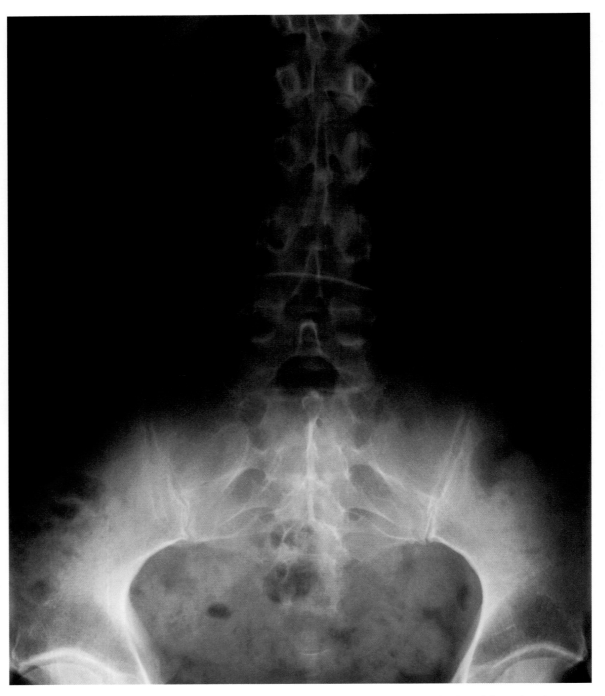

X-rays will reveal if broken bones or foreign objects are lodged in a body.

through the body before it exited the body or came to rest inside the body, which helps the medical examiner locate and extract bullets and their fragments when he does the internal exam.

The medical examiner looks for blunt-force trauma—injuries made with a blunt object. Hand and finger impressions may leave bruises. He measures these impressions to estimate hand and finger size. Old bruises as well as very recent ones that have not yet come to the surface of the skin may not be visible to the naked eye, but fortunately ultraviolet light illuminates them for inspection. If the medical examiner finds old or very new bruises, he or a professional photographer documents them under ultraviolet light. Bruises and injuries to the surface of the skin are nonpenetrating injuries.

When the medical examiner has finished "checking in" the body, collecting trace evidence, photographing, describing, measuring, and counting injuries, and has sent all of the evidence from the external examination to the forensics laboratory, he prepares for the internal examination. A tray of surgical tools will be ready near the sink and the autopsy table on which the body lies. From this tray he will select the appropriate tool, most likely a scalpel, to make the first incision that begins the internal autopsy.

The First Incision

On April 6, 1922, Jennie Becker and her husband Abraham went to a party at a friend's home in New York City. At the party, Jennie ate many of the delicacies offered: meat-spread canapés, grapes, figs, and almonds. The couple, whose marriage was less than happy, left the party. Jennie was never seen again.

When police investigated Jennie's disappearance, Abraham Becker claimed his wife left the party with another man. Police next questioned Reuben Norkin, one of Abraham Becker's colleagues. Norkin did not hold up long under such heated inquiry and told police he had helped Becker bury his wife in a shallow grave. He claimed Becker killed his wife with a wrench and buried her in a grave sprinkled with lime to cause her body to decompose more rapidly, and he even led police to the grave site.

The medical examiner, Dr. Karl Kennard, exhumed Jennie Becker's body for reexamination. Abraham Becker insisted the corpse could not belong to his wife because his wife was much larger than the corpse exhumed, and the clothes on the corpse did not match the clothes his wife wore to the party.

The medical examiner was certain the body belonged to Jennie Becker when he examined the stomach contents. Inside the stomach were meat-spread canapés, grapes, figs, and almonds. Still denying the body was his wife's, Abraham Becker claimed anyone could have eaten these foods, not just his wife. However, when the medical examiner tested the meat spread from the canapés, he found it matched the unique family recipe served at the party the night Jennie disappeared. The medical examiner's testimony later helped convict both Abraham Becker and Reuben Norkin of first-degree murder.

In many cases, a medical examiner must perform more than an external examination of a body to find out how, why, and when she died. Circumstances of the case may compel him to look inside the body, also. If the victim ate a certain combination of foods before she died, as Jennie Becker did, the medical examiner may be able to identify the body based on what he finds in the stomach. Or if he wants to find out if multiple, severe injuries to the outside of the body caused damage to internal organs, he may conduct a full autopsy of the victim, examining each organ of the body individually. A full autopsy takes about two hours.

The First Incision

After the external examination, the forensic pathologist chooses a scalpel and a pair of surgical scissors from her tray of sterilized instruments and

The Eight Important Organs Examined in an Autopsy

1. liver
2. spleen
3. stomach
4. pancreas

5. heart
6. lungs
7. brain
8. skin

begins making a "Y" incision. She makes the incision from each shoulder to the breastbone and down the center of the body to the pubic bone, pulling back the skin to expose the liver and intestines. With a bone saw, she cuts through the ribs and collarbone to remove the breastplate and reveal the heart and lungs.

With a needle, the forensic pathologist collects bodily fluids for toxicological (drugs and toxins) and serological (blood) analyses. She sends urine samples from the bladder, bile from the gallbladder, blood from the heart, and vitreous humor from the eyes to the forensics laboratory, where technicians will look for drugs, alcohol, and other chemicals in the fluids. Blood from the heart is also important for DNA analysis when the identity of the deceased is unknown.

After she sends the fluids to the laboratory, the forensic pathologist removes the heart, lungs, liver, pancreas, and spleen. Once she has weighed each of these organs, she examines the contents of the stomach for food, pills, and any evidence of other toxins. With scissors, she opens the stom-

Case Study:
A Deadly Doctor

Michael Swango was charming, blond, young, athletic, and charismatic. From his appearance, the medical intern at the Ohio State University Medical Center seemed to be a competent doctor, but before the end of his internship, five patients died under his care, and many coworkers became ill. Nurses who worked with Swango noticed his patients' health would stabilize after they arrived at the hospital, but every time Swango returned from the patients' bedsides, their conditions would rapidly decline.

Cynthia McGee was just such a case. The gymnast with Olympic promise survived being hit by a car only to end up under Swango's care at Ohio State University. Reviewing her medical records and autopsy report years after her death, a forensic pathologist learned toxicology tests showed lethal levels of potassium in her blood. Swango had poisoned her, but the test results went unnoticed. Staff continued to be suspicious of Swango's bedside manner, but the hospital administration paid little attention to their concerns. Authorities even investigated Swango for murder once his internship ended, but failed to find evidence worthy of a conviction. Meanwhile, Swango had already moved on to another job with fresh victims.

While working as a paramedic after his medical internship, Swango's coworkers caught him trying to poison them. This, and the store of poison in his locker, helped authorities convict him of aggravated assault. Unfortunately, the conviction did not stop him from killing. Swango was practicing medicine again after less than three years in prison.

In South Dakota, Virginia, New York, and even Zimbabwe, more of Swango's patients died, and more of his coworkers got sick after eating a "home-cooked meal" he made for them. A forensic pathologist later exhumed the bodies of some of Swango's victims to find out how they died. Based on reports from surviving victims that Swango had injected a solution into their IVs that made them unable to move, the forensic pathologist submitted fluids from the bodies to a toxicology lab. Test reports confirmed what the forensic pathologist, surviving victims, and Swango's former coworkers suspected: Swango had indeed poisoned his patients.

Swango deceived and charmed his way into seven more hospitals before the FBI finally caught up with him. By this time, he had murdered between thirty-five and sixty patients in fewer than two decades. In September of 2000, with the help of toxicology reports and expert testimony from the forensic pathologist and toxicologists, a grand jury sentenced Swango to life in prison without parole.

ach over the sink and lets the contents fill a storage container. She will send the container and its contents to the laboratory, and may also send the contents of the intestines along with those of the stomach. Forensic pathology technicians use microscopes to examine tissue samples from all the organs the forensic pathologist inspects. They carry out histological (tissue) investigations for evidence of disease and trauma, and microbiological analyses to look for infectious biological agents.

The organs in the abdominal cavity and pelvis are the next ones to be examined. The forensic pathologist removes the bladder and internal reproductive organs, the kidneys, adrenal glands, aorta, and any other soft tissues and fluids. When the body cavity is clear of obstructions, she examines the space for any irregularities. If she finds something out of the ordinary, a police or medical photographer photographs it.

The last organ the forensic pathologist examines is the brain. To access it, the forensic pathologist peels back the scalp and opens the skull with a handsaw. She first weighs the brain, rinses blood from it, and examines its surface for abnormalities, most often hemorrhages but also tumors. After looking inside and outside the skull, the forensic pathologist cuts the brain to search for internal evidence of **hemorrhaging**. The photographer takes a photograph of any evidence of trauma to the brain. Once the forensic pathologist examines the organs of the neck, the autopsy is done. She places all of the discarded organs into a plastic biohazard bag inside the body cavity, sews up the body, and returns to her office to write a report about the autopsy. The family of the deceased can then make burial arrangements.

The Autopsy Report

After the forensic pathologist finishes the autopsy and reviews the toxicology results from the laboratory, she uses her autopsy chart to write an autopsy report that she will send to the law enforcement agency investigating the case. The report discusses her conclusions and opinions about the circumstances surrounding the person's death. This legal document is a record of her observations, which she can review any time in the future. She may be asked to present this report in a court of law, sometimes years after the initial autopsy, so the report must be as detailed and accurate as possible.

The forensic pathologist includes basic information in the report such as the victim's name, age, sex, address, and profession; the location, date, and time of the autopsy; the name of the forensic pathologist; and the authority requesting the autopsy. She must report her findings on the time of death, the probable sequence of events leading up to the victim's death, and his cause of death. She discusses the observations she made during the external and internal examinations as well as results of laboratory tests. These results and observations justify her conclusions, which can make or break a criminal case.

The Death Certificate

A death certificate is a legal document reporting a person's immediate cause of death, any contributing causes of death, and manner of death. Anyone can view a death certificate belonging to another person because death certificates, like birth certificates, are public records.

The forensic pathologist writes a death certificate after reviewing all information in the case—the investigative reports and photographs from the crime scene or the place where the person died, police reports, medical records, results of the toxicological analysis, and her own findings from the autopsy report. If she is not a medical examiner, she submits the death certificate to a medical examiner or coroner, who approves of her conclusions and signs the death certificate. By law, a medical examiner or coroner must

United States of America - State of New Mexico - New Mexico Vital Records and Health Statistics.

CERTIFICATE OF DEATH - Certified by Medical Investigator ☐   Certified by Physician ☐

(NOTE: If death is due to accident, homicide, trauma, or unknown causes, refer case to Medical Investigator)

County of Death	City, Town, Location

DECEASED

DECEDENT - NAME	First	Middle	Last	SEX	DATE OF DEATH (mo, day, yr)
1.				2.	3.

DATE OF BIRTH (mo, day, yr)	AGE - last birthday	UNDER 1 YEAR MOS. DAYS	UNDER 1 DAY HOURS MINS.	RACE - Specify White, Black, Native American, etc.	IF NATIVE AMERICAN, Specify Tribal Affiliation (e.g. Zia, Jicarilla, Navajo, etc.)
4.	5a.	5b.	5c.	6a.	6b.

DECEDENT HISPANIC?   Spanish ☐   Mexican ☐   Cuban ☐   Puerto Rican ☐   Other ☐ Specify

6o. ☐ NO   ☐ Yes Specify:

EDUCATION OF DECEDENT - Indicate highest grade completed   7. 0 1 2 3 4 5 6 7 8 9 10 11 12 13 14 15 16 17 + UNK

PLACE OF DEATH - Name of hospital or other facility (if neither, give street and number or location)

8a.

HOSPITAL	☐ Inpatient	☐ ER/Outpatient	☐ DOA	OTHER	☐ Nursing Home	☐ Residence	☐ Other (Specify)
8b.							

STATE OR COUNTRY OF BIRTH	CITIZEN OF WHAT COUNTRY	MARRIED, NEVER MARRIED, WIDOWED, DIVORCED - Specify	SURVIVING SPOUSE (If wife, give birth name)	WAS DECEDENT EVER IN U.S. ARMED FORCES?
9.	10.	11.	12.	13. ☐ YES ☐ NO

SOCIAL SECURITY NUMBER	USUAL OCCUPATION (Kind of work done during most of working life, even if retired)	KIND OF BUSINESS OR INDUSTRY
14.	15a.	15b.

RESIDENCE - State	County	City, Town or Location	INSIDE CITY LIMITS?
16a.	16b.	16c.	16d. ☐ YES ☐ NO

STREET AND NUMBER OR LOCATION	ZIP CODE
16c.	16f.

PARENTS

FATHER - NAME First	Middle	Last	MOTHER - BIRTH NAME First	Middle	Last
17.			18.		

INFORMANT - NAME (Type or print)	MAILING ADDRESS Street/RFD No.	City/Town	State	Zip
19a.	19b.			

DISPOSITION

METHOD OF DISPOSITION   ☐ Burial ☐ Cremation ☐ Removal from State ☐ Donation ☐ Entombment ☐ Other (Specify)

20a.

CEMETERY/CREMATORY - Name   20b.

LOCATION	City/Town	State	FUNERAL SERVICE LICENSEE or PERSON ACTING AS SUCH - Signature	LICENSE NUMBER
20c.			21a. ▶	21b.

FACILITY - NAME	FACILITY - ADDRESS Street/RFD No.	City/Town	State
21c.	21d.		

CERTIFICATION

CERTIFIER'S SIGNATURE - On the basis of examination and/or investigation, in my opinion death occurred at the time, date and place and due to the cause(s) stated.

☐ Office of Medical Investigator ☐ Tribal/Military Authority ☐ Certified Physician

DATE SIGNED (mo, day, yr)	HOUR OF DEATH
22c.	22d.

PRONOUNCED DEAD (mo, day, yr)	PRONOUNCED DEAD (hour)
22e.	22f.

22a. ▶

TYPE/PRINT NAME   22b.

ADDRESS

MANNER OF DEATH   22g.   ☐ NATURAL   ☐ ACCIDENT   ☐ SUICIDE   ☐ HOMICIDE   ☐ UNDETERMINED

DATE FILED AT NMVRHS (mo, day, yr)	STATE REGISTRAR'S SIGNATURE
23a.	23b.

CAUSE OF DEATH

WAS AN AUTOPSY PERFORMED?	If yes, were findings considered in determining cause of death?	LOCATION WHERE AUTOPSY WAS PERFORMED (CITY, STATE)
24a. ☐ YES ☐ NO	24b. ☐ YES ☐ NO	24c.

WAS RECENT SURGICAL PROCEDURE PERFORMED?	IF YES, SPECIFY TYPE OF PROCEDURE	DATE OF PROCEDURE	WAS DECEDENT PREGNANT WITHIN LAST 6 WEEKS?	If yes, estimated length of pregnancy
25a. ☐ YES ☐ NO	25b.	25c.	26a. ☐ YES ☐ NO	26b.

DESCRIBE HOW INJURY OCCURRED (COMPLETE FOR ACCIDENT, SUICIDE, HOMICIDE, UNDETERMINED)	HOUR OF INJURY	DATE OF INJURY - (mo, day, yr)
27a.	27b.	27c.

INJURY AT WORK	PLACE OF INJURY - Specify home, farm, street, etc.	LOCATION	Street/RFD No.	City/Town	State
27d. ☐ YES ☐ NO	27e.	27f.			

TYPE OR PRINT CLEARLY   PLEASE PRESS FIRMLY - MULTIPLE COPIES BEING MADE

28.   PART I. Enter the diseases, injuries or complications which caused the death. Do not enter the mode of dying, such as cardiac or respiratory arrest, shock, or heart failure. List only one cause per each line.

Approximate interval between onset and death

IMMEDIATE CAUSE (Final disease or condition resulting in death.)   a. _____ DUE TO (OR AS A CONSEQUENCE OF):

Sequentially list conditions, if any, leading to immediate cause. Enter UNDERLYING CAUSE (Disease or injury which initiated events resulting in death) LAST   b. _____ DUE TO (OR AS A CONSEQUENCE OF):

c. _____ DUE TO (OR AS A CONSEQUENCE OF):

d. _____

PART II. Other significant conditions contributing to death but not resulting in the underlying cause given in Part I.

SHADED AREAS FOR MEDICAL INVESTIGATOR - LEGAL OFFICER USE ONLY

NMVRHS 904 REV. 3/99

A death certificate is completed by the medical examiner.

issue a death certificate within seventy-two hours of a person's death in the United States and within forty-eight hours in Canada.

The medical examiner or coroner may only partially complete the death certificate if he has not received the results of laboratory tests within the forty-eight- or seventy-two-hour period. Without evidence from toxicological, radiological, and histological analyses, among others, she cannot make a complete conclusion about the mechanism, cause, manner, and time of death.

Completing the autopsy report and death certificate is the last step of the medical examiner or forensic pathologist's job before she testifies in court. At this stage she has collected evidence from the body and possibly the crime scene, sent specimens to the laboratory for analyses, and interpreted laboratory results. Her job does not, however, involve delivering an opinion about the guilt or innocence of a suspect. Once she completes the autopsy report and death certificate, detectives use them to reconstruct the circumstances surrounding the victim's death, find a suspect, and arrest him if the evidence warrants it. The methods the medical examiner uses to determine when, how, and why a person died are critical to the investigation that will continue beyond the morgue.

410-676-03   410-676-04   4

6

The Cold Hard Facts: Victim Identity and Time of Death

One cold, crisp February day, a young man chased a rabbit into a clearing, but instead of catching it, he stumbled upon the body of a boy. The boy was malnourished, horribly beaten, and wrapped in a blanket inside a furniture box.

When a forensic scientist examined the remains, he knew the boy was no older than six years. He knew severe head trauma from multiple blows caused his death, but he could not determine the time of death or the boy's identity.

Several pieces of evidence might have revealed the child's identity—the distinctive print on the blanket, the furniture box from a local store in Fox Chase,

Pennsylvania, a man's personalized cap near the scene, and some unique scars and moles on the boy's body—but none of these clues provided a promising lead. Authorities buried the body, and the case remained open for more than twenty years.

Then, in 1998, the Vidocq Society, a group of forensic scientists and law enforcement personnel based in Pennsylvania and devoted to working together on unsolved criminal cases, took on the mysterious case of "The Boy in the Box."

Police who worked for several years on the case found a breakthrough lead that took them to a woman and her psychiatrist. Police interviewed the woman, who told them the story of a traumatic childhood.

In the mid-1950s, the woman's abusive mother adopted a toddler she named Jonathan. Her parents kept the child in a furniture box in the basement. One day, her mother killed the child when she beat his head on the bathroom floor. The woman recalled the blanket and furniture box her mother put him in before dumping his body, and told police her mother cut his hair and she herself clipped his nails after he died. Sure enough, investigators examining the body twenty years earlier had found the boy's nails and hair recently cut.

The Vidocq Society took DNA samples from the boy's body, which matched the DNA of the woman the police interviewed. At last, the "boy in the box" had a name. The evidence the forensic pathologist collected from the boy's autopsy helped determine his identity and the manner and cause of his death. Trace evidence obtained from the external examination of his body—hairs on the blanket—was key to confirming the woman investigators interviewed did indeed witness the boy's murder.

A forensic pathologist uses many clues to determine when, why, and how a person died, and these clues may come from the external or the internal autopsy, or both.

Identifying the Victim

Identifying the victim can be relatively simple if the medical examiner has a fresh, intact body to examine. If scars, tattoos, old injuries, and piercings on the corpse match those of the victim, then he can be reasonably sure the corpse belongs to the victim. The medical examiner may be able to

Medical examiners distinguish between animal bones and human bones.

match the corpse's injuries to those of the victim during the autopsy. DNA extracted from blood samples may confirm the identity of the corpse if her DNA matches the DNA of the victim or that of the victim's family members. However, medical examiners work on many cases in which the body has already decomposed so much that the skin where identifying marks would be is gone, and the internal organs that tell the story of deadly injuries have disappeared. In this case, a forensic anthropologist helps the medical examiner determine the corpse's identity from her bones. Most medical examiners can distinguish human bones from the bones of animals and may be able to identify the sex of the corpse. Beyond this point, a forensic anthropologist will be able to determine the age, build, and ancestry of the corpse as well as any injuries she may have suffered. Instead of collecting DNA from the blood cells, a forensic anthropologist may collect mitochondrial DNA from hair and bones.

Time of Death

Estimating a victim's time of death is one of the more tricky tasks a forensic pathologist faces because many variables affect the reliability of his estimation. A forensic pathologist considers several postmortem changes in the body to determine time of death. Some of these changes are:

- body temperature
- rigor mortis
- livor mortis
- decomposition stage
- stomach contents

Case Study:
The Royal Romanov Family

During World War I, Lenin forced Czar Nicholas II of Russia to give up his throne and placed the czar, his family, and servants under house arrest in Siberia. On July 16, 1918, Bolsheviks forced them into the basement of the house, where they shot and killed the czar, his wife, five children, family physician, and three servants. When their attempt to burn the bodies in a mine shaft failed, soldiers poured acid on them to make them decompose faster. Soldiers removed nine of the bodies and buried them in a different location, where they remained until a team of forensic scientists exhumed them in 1992.

The discovery of a mass grave raised the suspicion that the bones inside belonged to the czar and his family, so a forensic anthropologist, a forensic dentist, a forensic trace analyst, and a forensic pathologist investigated the remains to determine whether they were indeed those of the royal Romanov family. Luckily, the forensic pathologist found two bullets in what little tissue was left on one of the skeletons. The bullets dated back to World War I, which indicated the cache of bones was likely the remains of the Romanov family.

The medical examiner takes the victim's rectal or liver temperature and compares this temperature with that of the victim's surroundings to estimate time of death. After death, the human body cools to the temperature of its environment at a rate of 1.5 degrees per hour. The medical examiner uses this rate to calculate how long the victim has been dead.

However, many factors influence body temperature. A body loses heat more slowly inside a house than in a freezer, for example. Changes in the temperature of a body's surroundings, such as intense sunlight followed by a cold night, may slow and speed up the rate at which the body loses heat. The condition of the body before death also affects its rate of cooling. For example, an obese person or a person wearing heavy clothing loses heat at a slower rate than a very thin person or a person without clothing.

Rigor mortis—the postmortem stiffening of muscles—helps the medical examiner or forensic pathologist estimate time of death because rigor occurs in a predictable pattern at a rate dependant on the environment around the corpse. At seventy degrees Fahrenheit (21 degrees Celsius):

1. Two hours after death: small muscles in the face and neck stiffen, and rigor works its way down into the large muscles from head to toe.
2. Eight to twelve hours after death: full rigor mortis sets in.
3. Eighteen hours after death: rigor mortis becomes fixed.
4. Rigor mortis reverses in the same order in which it began.
5. Twelve hours later, rigor disappears and all muscles relax.

The trouble with rigor mortis is that the medical examiner can only use it to estimate time of death within a thirty-six- to forty-eight-hour window of the victim's demise. Also, temperature makes estimating time of death

What Makes a Stiff, Stiff?

To go about our everyday lives, we rely on muscle contractions to help move our legs, arms, hands, and countless other body parts. Muscles require energy to contract, and the energy currency they use is a compound called adenosine triphosphate (ATP). To make ATP, the body needs oxygen. When a person dies, oxygen circulation stops, and so does the supply of ATP to the muscles. Without ATP, muscles become rigid because they are in a state of contraction.

In warmer environments, muscles consume ATP at a higher rate. So, if a person dies of a fever or infection that raises body temperature, or uses up much ATP by expending a lot of energy just before death, signs of rigor mortis will appear in muscles much sooner after death. In someone who ran from an attacker, for example, the first signs of rigor will occur in the legs where muscles used the most energy. Similarly, rigor sets in faster in a victim who has tried to fight his attacker.

difficult because heat, whether from the environment or generated by the victim's body, speeds up the process.

Livor mortis—the pooling of blood in blood vessels—also occurs in a predictable pattern that allows the medical examiner to estimate time of death.

Additionally, it indicates if someone moved the victim. Livor mortis causes skin to turn red or purplish shortly after death. The parts of the body touching a surface, however, look pale because the pressure of the body on the vessels causes blood to pool away from points of contact. For example, if a victim lies face down, his face, shoulders, stomach, knees, and any other parts of the underside of his body will be pale.

Livor mortis appears within thirty minutes of death and becomes permanent between six and eight hours later. Usually, blood still shifts with movement of the body six hours after death. The medical examiner can see that someone moved the victim from the original position in which he died because his body will have the dark purple tint of full livor mortis in some

If a victim dies lying face down, her face and the underside of her body will be pale.

areas and also the faint purple or red shade of early livor mortis in others. If the victim died on his back but the perpetrator moved him to his side to stage the crime scene about four hours later, the victim's face, torso, and the fronts of his legs and arms would have a slight red or purple tint from lying on his back before livor mortis became fixed. The rest of his body, excluding the side of his face, arm, hips, and legs in contact with the floor, would be a dark red or purple from fixed livor mortis. If a victim dies lying on an object, such as a license plate, the object will leave an impression in white on the victim's skin, which the medical examiner can use to link a suspect with the victim. The color of livor mortis may also indicate the cause of death. Victims who die of strangulation, for example, are purple, due to low oxygen in their blood.

The more gory details of the body also help the medical examiner determine a rough estimate of time of death. Decomposition—the breaking down of tissues—also takes place in a predictable pattern and rate depending on environmental conditions such as temperature, humidity, and exposure to insects and other scavenging animals. The medical examiner can also look at the condition of internal organs, where decomposition begins with the intestines and finishes with the liver, lungs, brain, kidneys, and stomach. If he finds the intestines decomposed but the lungs intact, he can be fairly sure the victim died recently.

Forensic scientists who study decomposition break the process into stages:

1. Within thirty-six hours after death, the abdomen, neck, shoulders, and head turn green.
2. Bacteria in the body release gas as they break down tissues, causing the body to bloat from the face down.
3. Liquid accumulates over large areas of the skin.
4. The skin marbles, or shows blood vessels as red blood cells break down and stain the vessel walls.

The Cold Hard Facts: Victim Identity and Time of Death　　**91**

Case Study: Bill Bass and the Body Farm

The Body Farm is a two-and-one-half-acre (1 hectare) research facility at the University of Tennessee in Knoxville. Research on the farm has been critical to estimating a victim's time of death. At any given time, forty bodies in various conditions decompose in this field. Bodies lie submerged in ponds, stuffed in the trunks of cars, buried under debris or even several feet under ground. Some are whole, others are in pieces. The purpose of this grisly experiment: to solve heinous crimes by understanding human decomposition just a little bit better.

Bill Bass, the scientist who created the Body Farm, is a forensic anthropologist and professor of anthropology at the University of Tennessee. Dr. Bass has been working on homicides, burials, and disaster cases for almost fifty years. His job is to work with forensic odontologists to help the medical examiner find out the identity, age, sex, build, and ancestry of human bones and decomposed remains. Dr. Bass is an expert at reading human bones, but he is also no stranger to the more recently deceased.

While working as a consultant for the Kansas Bureau of Investigation, a cattle rustling case gave Dr. Bass the idea for the Body Farm. Asked to determine the time of death of one of the cows from its bones, Dr. Bass was stumped. At the time, little research into using the decomposition process to calculate time of death existed. He realized he needed to kill a cow and study its decomposition to answer the question.

Dr. Bass understood the same problem existed with investigating deaths of human beings. He determined scientific observations of human decomposition were necessary but found less than enthusiastic support for his idea. Finally, in 1971, the University of Tennessee donated land to the project, and Dr. Bass planted it with the unclaimed bodies of homeless men. Today, the Body Farm, otherwise known as the University of Tennessee Anthropology Research Facility, is a teaching center for crime-scene investigators, forensic pathologists, and FBI agents. Law enforcement agents and other officials often simulate crime scenes to compare the decomposition rate of victims' bodies to that of simulations at the farm, hopefully coming closer to determining when, and sometimes where, the victim died.

5. The abdomen bloats, the skin continues to liquefy, and skin and hair slip from the body.
6. Purge fluid, the fluid of decomposition, drains from the mouth and nose and the body takes on a green-black color. Gases continue accumulating inside the body until the skin splits and releases gas and purge fluid.

Stomach contents give the forensic pathologist an estimate of time of death because food leaves the stomach every four to six hours, depending on the size and nutritional contents of the meal, and the rate at which

The Cold Hard Facts: Victim Identity and Time of Death **93**

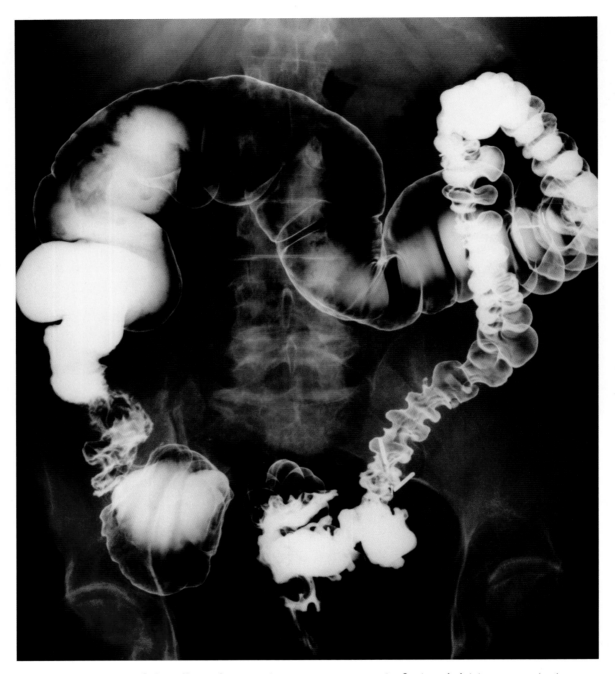

The contents of the digestive-system organs empty forty-eight to seventy-two hours after death.

each individual person digests food. A victim who died within a few hours of eating will still have undigested food in her stomach. If the stomach is completely empty, the victim probably died many hours after eating. The small intestine empties about twenty-four hours after eating, and the colon empties after forty-eight to seventy-two hours. So if the forensic pathologist finds the stomach, small intestine, and colon empty, he estimates the victim died forty-eight to seventy-two hours after her last meal.

The forensic pathologist will compare his time of death estimates from the autopsy with evidence from the crime scene, such as clocks or watches broken during an attack, to make his final estimate.

Once the forensic pathologist knows who the victim is and when she died, he begins uncovering clues that finish telling the story of the victim's death. Finding out how and why the victim died helps determine the person responsible for her death and just how responsible he is, depending on the type and severity of the injuries and which injuries ultimately caused the victim's death.

Reconstructing the Crime

Injuries to the skin, internal organs, and bones, and unusual changes in the body lead the forensic pathologist to discover how and why the victim died. Fracture patterns, carbon monoxide in a blood sample, and hemorrhages in the blood vessels of the eyes all suggest different circumstances leading up to a victim's death. Fortunately, the forensic pathologist can scrutinize the fine details of cuts, bruises, and bumps like no other scientist can.

Reading Injuries

The medical examiner can determine much about the cause and manner of death from the pattern, distribution, location, size, and kinds of injuries to the body. Gunshot and stab wounds, scrapes, and bruises can all result in homicidal, suicidal, and accidental death. The medical examiner's job is to describe and measure wounds to find out how they actually occurred. Some typical injury patterns and the circumstances in which they occur are:

GUNSHOT WOUNDS

Gunshot wounds occur in suicides, homicides, and accidental deaths. Characteristics of entrance wounds where the bullet entered the victim's body indicate the distance between the victim and the muzzle of the gun, which can narrow down the manner of death when combined with other evidence. A bullet from a gun fired more than two feet (.6 meters) away from the victim leaves a small, clean entrance wound with black-and-blue bruising around it where the bullet tore through the skin. A muzzle held to the victim's skin leaves a star-shaped pattern with gas and other particles embedded in the skin around the wound. In both cases, the manner of death may be homicide or suicide.

STAB, CUT, AND CHOP WOUNDS

Stab wounds are usually homicidal. From the wound's width, depth, and appearance, and the impression the handle leaves on the skin, the medical examiner can identify the type of weapon, for instance a weapon with a straight versus a serrated blade.

Cut wounds are typically suicidal but may be homicidal, too. Several shallow slices combined with one deeper, fatal slice to the wrist indicate suicide because the victim made hesitation wounds while building up courage to make the final cut. Homicidal cut wounds commonly occur on a victim's neck. The length and direction of a cut reveals the position of the killer and whether he is left- or right-handed. A killer standing behind the victim makes a long cut from ear to ear, but a killer in front of a victim makes a short cut across the neck. Right-handed killers cut from left to right; left-handed killers cut from right to left. Additionally, a victim who fought her attacker will have defensive wounds—cuts received while trying to fight off an attacker. These cuts occur on a victim's hands, wrists, and forearms.

Chop wounds are mainly accidental and caused by sharp, heavy objects such as axes or cleavers. The object usually leaves a wedge-shaped wound and cuts into and fractures the bone beneath it.

BRUISES

Bruises, or contusions, occur inside and outside the body when vessels leak blood into the tissues. Most bruises seen in criminal investigations are

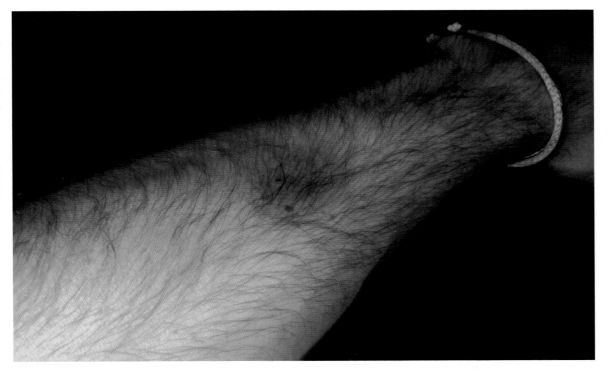

Examiners can determine when bruises were inflicted because they fade in predictable ways.

homicidal, but some are also accidental. A strangulation victim may have impressions of the killer's fingers on her neck that the medical examiner can measure for the size of the killer's hands. Bruises may also identify the type of weapon that made them if it leaves an impression on the victim's skin. Organs such as the spleen and liver can suffer traumatic bruising the medical examiner can only see in an internal exam. This sort of injury occurs in severe assaults and vehicle accidents. The medical examiner determines the age of bruises and looks for repeat abuse. Also, he can determine whether bite marks occurred before or after death by the age of the bruises they created. The age of bruises can be estimated because they fade in a predictable way: from dark to light blue, then green-yellow to brownish-yellow, usually within fourteen days. When a bruise fades, the loss of color is actually due to the body's own system of housekeeping: cells called **macrophages** eat up remnants of the red blood cells leaked into the tissues.

SCRAPES

Scrapes, or abrasions, occur in homicides, suicides, and accidents. A victim of smothering, in which the attacker suffocates him with a pillow or other item, often has abrasions around the nose and mouth. The item used to suffocate him may leave a unique imprint that allows the medical examiner to track down the murder weapon and collect the killer's DNA from it. Abrasions or contusions to a victim's scalp are important clues because they indicate blunt-force head trauma that most likely caused bleeding in the brain and, eventually, death.

BONE FRACTURES

The medical examiner can determine the age of fractures because fractures heal in a predictable way over the course of about five months. If she sees

Case Study:
Senseless Murder

Working in a coroner's office in Pennsylvania, Dr. Ladham never knows what kinds of cases will await him each morning. On his way to the autopsy room, he reads the death investigation report and scans the crime-scene photographs. This time the victim is a six-month-old girl, and case evidence suggests infanticide.

When her father did not drop her off at day care that morning, employees became worried and called his home. No one answered the telephone, so they called the police. Fifteen minutes later, police found the girl dead in her bedroom, where blood spatter covered her bed and the ceiling above it. According to the crime-scene investigator, the girl had suffered head trauma. Another detective informs Dr. Ladham that the girl's parents are in the middle of a bitter divorce.

Dr. Ladham retrieves the child's body from the refrigerator and begins the autopsy. He examines her head and finds multiple abrasions to the scalp and underlying circular fractures in the shape of a hammer. Dr. Ladham concludes the girl died of multiple blows to the head with this weapon. He signs a death certificate listing "homicide" as the manner of death and asks the detectives attending the autopsy to look for the weapon at the crime scene.

multiple fractures, both old and recent, on a victim's X-ray, she will conclude the victim suffered prolonged abuse before dying. The age of fractures also helps her pinpoint the blow that might have caused the victim's demise. The type of fracture tells the medical examiner about the direction and sequence of blows the victim suffered and possibly what delivered the blows. Crush fractures, where an object's direct force leaves several fracture lines in the bone, often occur in pedestrians struck by cars, for instance. The shape of fractures may reveal the type of weapon that inflicted the blows.

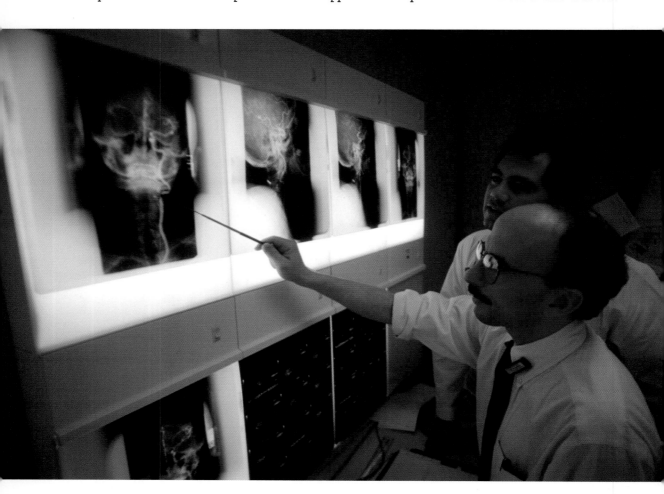

X-rays help reveal the type of trauma that led to the victim's death.

Drowning is a common cause of death.

Circular fractures of the skull may come from a hammer or a pipe, which investigators may retrieve from the crime scene. DNA from the weapon can place the perpetrator with the victim at the time of the crime.

Common Causes of Death

Medical examiners know to look for certain changes in the human body that indicate various causes of death such as drowning, strangulation, and electrocution. Here are just a few of the common causes of death medical examiners deal with, and clues to look for:

DROWNING

Determining whether a victim drowned is a difficult problem for the medical examiner because victims killed on dry land and dumped in water are very similar to victims who actually drowned when it comes to the autopsy. For example, both victims may have fluid in their lungs. However, medical examiners know to look for a few clues that can point to a drowning death. He expects to find bleeding in the lungs and sinuses of a drowning victim because the lack of oxygen puts pressure on these organs. He also expects to find debris from the water the victim would have inhaled in her fight to breathe. He uses other evidence in the case unrelated to the autopsy to make a final conclusion, but most drownings turn out to be accidental.

STRANGULATION

Strangulation causes capillaries in the eyes to rupture and leak blood. These leakages appear as fine red streaks or tiny dots called petechial hemorrhages. Pressure in the veins of the neck rises rapidly and sharply, bursting the capillaries. Injuries such as bruises and abrasions where the attacker's fingers and fingernails dug into the skin may occur on the victim's neck. Medical examiners often find fractures of the Adam's apple and bleeding in the small muscles of the neck from the force of the attack. In cases where a perpetrator uses an object to strangle his victim, the pressure of the object may leave marks on the neck that can help the medical examiner identify the weapon.

ELECTROCUTION

The signs of electrocution are unique if not bizarre. For one, rigor mortis occurs earliest on one side of the body. If a person touches an exposed

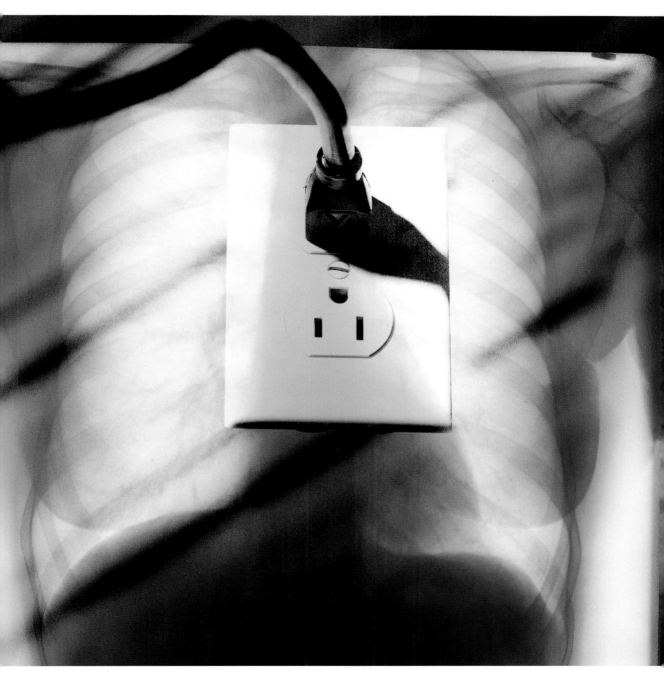

High-voltage electrocutions will char internal organs.

wire with one hand, the current passes through that hand and exits the body from the foot on the same side of her body. Rigor mortis sets in more rapidly on this side of the body because the electric current causes muscle contractions that use up ATP. In high-voltage cases, the current will char the hand that touched the wire, and the medical examiner may find the internal organs severely burned. Low-voltage currents, however, leave little if any clues for the medical examiner, and she may conclude such a victim died of an unknown cause.

These are just some of the types of cases a medical examiner often sees. His expertise in medicine and pathology allows him to diagnose when, how, and why a person died, which can connect the murder weapon to the victim or suspect, place the suspect with the victim before he died, and at the most basic level, identify victims of foul play, the murder weapon involved, and the scene where the crime occurred. All this evidence can make or break a legal case.

Many crime series like *CSI* and *Cold Case* romanticize the forensic pathologist's role in crime-solving—the haggard figure in white protective wear whisking into a crime scene, examining the victim with great zeal, and somehow coming up with the circumstances of his death before the commercial break. She crawls through abandoned mine shafts and creepy old buildings to retrieve and examine the bodies of victims for the greater good. Part of this portrayal is true. A forensic pathologist is adventurous and courageous, investigating scenes of violence most people cannot imagine. She may at times risk her life to collect evidence. A forensic pathologist is remarkable because she dares to tread "where death rejoices to help the living." Indeed, forensic pathology rests on the foundation of over seven hundred years of advancement in medicine that has been the work of early scholars, doctors, and artists alike, and continues to grow and develop in laboratories worldwide.

Glossary

ballistics: The study of the movements and forces involved in the propulsion of objects through the air.

entomologists: Scientists who study insects.

genetics: The hereditary makeup of an organism.

hemorrhage: The loss of blood from a ruptured blood vessel, either internally or externally.

macrophages: Any of the large phagocytic cells of the reticuloendothelial system.

medico-legal: Relating to both medicine and law.

mitochondria: A spherical or elongated organelle in the cytoplasm of nearly all eukaryotic cells, containing genetic material and many enzymes important for cell metabolism.

postmortem: Occurring after death.

protocol: The detailed plan of a scientific procedure.

subdural: Beneath the dura matter that covers the brain and spinal cord.

vitreous humor: The fluid component of the gel that fills the main cavity of the eye between the lens and retina.

Further Reading

Bass, W. M., and Jon Jefferson. *Death's Acre: Inside the Legendary Forensic Lab*. New York: Putnam Publishing Group, 2003.

Camenson, B. *Opportunities in Forensic Science Careers*. New York: McGraw-Hill, 2009.

Craig, E. *Teasing Secrets from the Dead: My Investigations at America's Most Infamous Crime Scenes*. New York: Crown Publishers, 2004.

Evans, C. *The Casebook of Forensic Detection: How Science Solved 100 of the World's Most Baffling Crimes*. New York: Berkley Trade, 2007.

Genge, N. E. *The Forensic Casebook: The Science of Crime Scene Investigation*. New York: Ballantine Books, 2002.

Lee, H. *Famous Crimes Revisited: A Forensic Scientist Reexamines the Evidence*. New York: Berkley Publishing Group, 2004.

Ramsland, K. *The Science of Cold Case Files*. New York: Berkley Publishing Group, 2004.

Roach, M. *Stiff: The Curious Lives of Human Cadavers*. New York: W.W. Norton and Company, 2004.

For More Information

American Academy of Forensic Sciences
www.aafs.org

The American Journal of Forensic Medicine and Pathology
www.amjforensicmedicine.com

The Body Farm at the University of Tennessee
web.utk.edu/~anthrop

Federal Bureau of Investigation Forensics Laboratory
www.fbi.gov/hq/lab/labhome.htm

The National Association of Medical Examiners
www.thename.org

National Forensics Academy
www.nfa.tennessee.edu

Searchable Crime Library
www.crimelibrary.com

Young Forensic Scientists Forum
yfsf.aafs.org

Publisher's note:
The websites listed on this page were active at the time of publication. The publisher is not responsible for websites that have changed their addresses or discontinued operation since the date of publication. The publisher will review and update the website list upon each reprint.

Index

accidental death 32, 98–100, 104
adenosine triphosphate (ATP) 89, 106
American Board of Pathology 41
autopsy 12, 15, 17, 58–60, 62–64, 71, 74, 75, 78–79, 81, 84, 95, 101, 104

Baden, Dr. Michael 38–39, 68–69
Bamberg Code 23
Body Farm 92–93
body handling (procedure at crime scene) 53, 55
Bundy, Ted 57–58
burking 14, 35

chain of custody 52–53
coroner 23, 25, 36, 46, 55, 79, 81, 101
critical questions 30–31

da Vinci, Leonardo 20–21
death certificates 79, 81, 101
decomposition 91, 92–93
DNA 10–12, 41, 52, 53, 60, 63, 66, 75, 84, 86, 100, 103

evidence 12–14, 18, 33, 43, 45–47, 49, 52, 55, 59–60, 62–65, 71, 78, 81, 98, 106
expert witness (definition) 43

forensic anthropologist 49, 86
forensic entomologist 55
forensic investigator 54
forensic odontologist 49
forensic palynologist 55
forensic pathologist (education and training) 40–41
forensic pathology 11, 12, 15–19, 41, 49, 51–52, 74–75, 78–79, 81

history 14, 15–19, 20–23, 25, 42, 61–62, 87
homicide 23, 29, 31, 33, 98, 100, 102, 104, 106

injuries (types of) 65, 69, 71, 97–100, 102–103

Kennedy assassination 68–69

lighting techniques 64, 71
Locard Exchange Principle (Dr. Edmund Locard) 15

medical-examiner system 25, 36,
Model Post-mortem Examinations Act of 1954 37
Morgagni, Giovanni Battista 17

photography 47, 49, 51, 58, 63, 68–69, 71, 78, 79, 101
Pickton, Robert 9–10
postmortem changes 19, 21, 60, 65, 86, 88–91, 93, 105–106

suicidal death 32–33, 98, 100
Swango, Michael 76–77

time of death 86, 88–91, 93, 95
Tz'u, Sung 21
types of death 31–33

victim identification 85–86
Vidocq Society (Vidocq, Eugene François) 42, 84

Picture Credits

Biographies

AUTHOR

Maryalice Walker grew up in Falmouth, Maine, and is an alumna of Smith College in Northampton, Massachusetts. She currently studies bat ecomorphology at the University of Cape Town, South Africa. Her research interests include the ecology and reproductive biology of flying animals. In her spare time, she enjoys writing, hiking, and spending time with her family.

SERIES CONSULTANTS

Carla Miller Noziglia is Senior Forensic Advisor for the U.S. Department of Justice, International Criminal Investigative Training Assistant Program. A Fellow of the American Academy of Forensic Sciences, Ms. Noziglia served as chair of the board of Trustees of the Forensic Science Foundation. Her work has earned her many honors and commendations, including Distinguished Fellow from the American Academy of Forensic Sciences (2003) and the Paul L. Kirk Award from the American Academy of Forensic Sciences Criminalistics Section. Ms. Noziglia's publications include *The Real Crime Lab* (coeditor, 2005), *So You Want to be a Forensic Scientist* (coeditor, 2003), and contributions to *Drug Facilitated Sexual Assault* (2001), *Convicted by Juries, Exonerated by Science: Case Studies in the Use of DNA* (1996), and the *Journal of Police Science* (1989). She is on the editorial board of the *Journal for Forensic Identification*.

Jay Siegel is Director of the Forensic and Investigative Sciences Program at Indiana University-Purdue University, Indianapolis and Chair of the Department of Chemistry and Chemical Biology. He holds a Ph.D. in Analytical Chemistry from George Washington University. He worked for three years at the Virginia Bureau of Forensic Sciences, analyzing drugs, fire residues, and trace evidence. From 1980 to 2004 he was professor of forensic chemistry and director of the forensic science program at Michigan State University in the School of Criminal Justice. Dr. Siegel has testified over 200 times as an expert witness in twelve states, Federal Court and Military Court. He is editor in chief of the *Encyclopedia of Forensic Sciences*, author of *Forensic Science: A Beginner's Guide and Fundamentals of Forensic Science*, and he has more than thirty publications in forensic science journals. Dr. Siegel was awarded the 2005 Paul Kirk Award for lifetime achievement in forensic science. In February 2009, he was named Distinguished Fellow by the American Academy of Forensic Sciences.